ACID RAIN

EARTH • AT • RISK

ACID RAIN

by Peter Tyson

Introduction by
Russell E. Train

Chairman of
the Board of Directors,
World Wildlife Fund and
The Conservation Foundation

CHELSEA HOUSE PUBLISHERS

new york   philadelphia

CHELSEA HOUSE PUBLISHERS
EDITOR-IN-CHIEF: Remmel Nunn
MANAGING EDITOR: Karyn Gullen Browne
COPY CHIEF: Mark Rifkin
PICTURE EDITOR: Adrian G. Allen
ART DIRECTOR: Maria Epes
ASSISTANT ART DIRECTOR: Noreen Romano
MANUFACTURING DIRECTOR: Gerald Levine
SYSTEMS MANAGER: Lindsey Ottman
PRODUCTION MANAGER: Joseph Romano
PRODUCTION COORDINATOR: Marie Claire Cebrián

EARTH AT RISK
Senior Editor: Jake Goldberg

Staff for *Acid Rain*
ASSOCIATE EDITOR: Karen Hammonds
SENIOR COPY EDITOR: Laurie Kahn
EDITORIAL ASSISTANT: Danielle Janusz
PICTURE RESEARCHER: Villette Harris
DESIGNER: Marjorie Zaum

3 5 7 9 8 6 4 2

Library of Congress Cataloging-in-Publication Data
Tyson, Peter.
    Acid rain/by Peter Tyson; introduction by Russell E. Train.
      p. cm.—(Earth at risk)
    Includes bibliographical references and index.
    Summary: Discusses the problem of acid rain, its causes, how
it spreads, and its devastating effects on the environment. Also
examines possible solutions to the problem.
    ISBN 0-7910-1577-7
        0-7910-1602-1 (pbk.)
    1. Acid rain—Environmental aspects—Juvenile literature.
2. Air quality management—Juvenile literature. [1. Acid rain.
2. Environmental protection.] I. Title. II. Series.   91-22227
TD195.44.T97 1992   CIP
363.73'86—dc20   AC

CONTENTS

INTRODUCTION

Russell E. Train

Administrator, Environmental Protection Agency, 1973 to
1977; Chairman of the Board of Directors, World Wildlife
Fund and The Conservation Foundation

There is a growing realization that human activities increasingly
are threatening the health of the natural systems that make life possible
on this planet. Humankind has the power to alter nature fundamentally,
perhaps irreversibly.

This stark reality was dramatized in January 1989 when *Time*
magazine named Earth the "Planet of the Year." In the same year, the
Exxon *Valdez* disaster sparked public concern over the effects of human
activity on vulnerable ecosystems when a thick blanket of crude oil
coated the shores and wildlife of Prince William Sound in Alaska. And,
no doubt, the 20th anniversary celebration of Earth Day in April 1990
renewed broad public interest in environmental issues still further. It is
no accident then that many people are calling the years between 1990
and 2000 the "Decade of the Environment."

And this is not merely a case of media hype, for the 1990s will
truly be a time when the people of the planet Earth learn the meaning of
the phrase "everything is connected to everything else" in the natural
and man-made systems that sustain our lives. This will be a period when
more people will understand that burning a tree in Amazonia adversely
affects the global atmosphere just as much as the exhaust from the cars
that fill our streets and expressways.

Central to our understanding of environmental issues is the
need to recognize the complexity of the problems we face and the

relationships between environmental and other needs in our society. Global warming provides an instructive example. Controlling emissions of carbon dioxide, the principal greenhouse gas, will involve efforts to reduce the use of fossil fuels to generate electricity. Such a reduction will include energy conservation and the promotion of alternative energy sources, such as nuclear and solar power.

The automobile contributes significantly to the problem. We have the choice of switching to more energy efficient autos and, in the longer run, of choosing alternative automotive power systems and relying more on mass transit. This will require different patterns of land use and development, patterns that are less transportation and energy intensive.

In agriculture, rice paddies and cattle are major sources of greenhouse gases. Recent experiments suggest that universally used nitrogen fertilizers may inhibit the ability of natural soil organisms to take up methane, thus contributing tremendously to the atmospheric loading of that gas—one of the major culprits in the global warming scenario.

As one explores the various parameters of today's pressing environmental challenges, it is possible to identify some areas where we have made some progress. We have taken important steps to control gross pollution over the past two decades. What I find particularly encouraging is the growing environmental consciousness and activism by today's youth. In many communities across the country, young people are working together to take their environmental awareness out of the classroom and apply it to everyday problems. Successful recycling and tree-planting projects have been launched as a result of these budding environmentalists who have committed themselves to a cleaner environment. Citizen action, activated by youthful enthusiasm, was largely responsible for the fast-food industry's switch from rainforest to domestic beef, for pledges from important companies in the tuna industry to use fishing techniques that would not harm dolphins, and for the recent announcement by the McDonald's Corporation to phase out polystyrene "clam shell" hamburger containers.

Despite these successes, much remains to be done if we are to make ours a truly healthy environment. Even a short list of persistent issues includes problems such as acid rain, ground-level ozone and smog, and airborne toxins; groundwater protection and nonpoint sources of pollution, such as runoff from farms and city streets; wetlands protection; hazardous waste dumps; and solid waste disposal, waste minimization, and recycling.

Similarly, there is an unfinished agenda in the natural resources area: effective implementation of newly adopted management plans for national forests; strengthening the wildlife refuge system; national park management, including addressing the growing pressure of development on lands surrounding the parks; implementation of the Endangered Species Act; wildlife trade problems, such as that involving elephant ivory; and ensuring adequate sustained funding for these efforts at all levels of government. All of these issues are before us today; most will continue in one form or another through the year 2000.

Each of these challenges to environmental quality and our health requires a response that recognizes the complex nature of the problem. Narrowly conceived solutions will not achieve lasting results. Often it seems that when we grab hold of one part of the environmental balloon, an unsightly and threatening bulge appears somewhere else.

The higher environmental issues arise on the national agenda, the more important it is that we are armed with the best possible knowledge of the economic costs of undertaking particular environmental programs and the costs associated with not undertaking them. Our society is not blessed with unlimited resources, and tough choices are going to have to be made. These should be informed choices.

All too often, environmental objectives are seen as at cross-purposes with other considerations vital to our society. Thus, environmental protection is often viewed as being in conflict with economic growth, with energy needs, with agricultural productions, and so on. The time has come when environmental considerations must be fully integrated into every nation's priorities.

One area that merits full legislative attention is energy efficiency. The United States is one of the least energy efficient of all the industrialized nations. Japan, for example, uses far less energy per unit of gross national product than the United States does. Of course, a country as large as the United States requires large amounts of energy for transportation. However, there is still a substantial amount of excess energy used, and this excess constitutes waste. More fuel efficient autos and home heating systems would save millions of barrels of oil, or their equivalent, each year. And air pollutants, including greenhouse gases, could be significantly reduced by increased efficiency in industry.

I suspect that the environmental problem that comes closest to home for most of us is the problem of what to do with trash. All over the world, communities are wrestling with the problem of waste disposal. Landfill sites are rapidly filling to capacity. No one wants a trash and garbage dump near home. As William Ruckelshaus, former EPA administrator and now in the waste management business, puts it, "Everyone wants you to pick up the garbage and no one wants you to put it down!"

At the present time, solid waste programs emphasize the regulation of disposal, setting standards for landfills, and so forth. In the decade ahead, we must shift our emphasis from regulating waste disposal to an overall reduction in its volume. We must look at the entire waste stream, including product design and packaging. We must avoid creating waste in the first place. To the greatest extent possible, we should then recycle any waste that is produced. I believe that, while most of us enjoy our comfortable way of life and have no desire to change things, we also know in our hearts that our "disposable society" has allowed us to become pretty soft.

Land use is another domestic issue that might well attract legislative attention by the year 2000. All across the United States, communities are grappling with the problem of growth. All too often, growth imposes high costs on the environment—the pollution of aquifers; the destruction of wetlands; the crowding of shorelines; the loss of wildlife habitat; and the loss of those special places, such as a historic structure or area, that give a community a sense of identity. It is worth noting that growth is not only the product of economic development but of population movement. By the year 2010, for example, experts predict that 75% of all Americans will live within 50 miles of a coast.

It is important to keep in mind that we are all made vulnerable by environmental problems that cross international borders. Of course, the most critical global conservation problems are the destruction of tropical forests and the consequent loss of their biological capital. Some scientists have calculated extinction rates as high as 11 species per hour. All agree that the loss of species has never been greater than at the present time; not even the disappearance of the dinosaurs can compare to today's rate of extinction.

In addition to species extinctions, the loss of tropical forests may represent as much as 20% of the total carbon dioxide loadings to the atmosphere. Clearly, any international approach to the problem of global warming must include major efforts to stop the destruction of forests and to manage those that remain on a renewable basis. Debt for nature swaps, which the World Wildlife Fund has pioneered in Costa Rica, Ecuador, Madagascar, and the Philippines, provide a useful mechanism for promoting such conservation objectives.

Global environmental issues inevitably will become the principal focus in international relations. But the single overriding issue facing the world community today is how to achieve a sustainable balance between growing human populations and the earth's natural systems. If you travel as frequently as I do in the developing countries of Latin America, Africa, and Asia, it is hard to escape the reality that expanding human populations are seriously weakening the earth's resource base. Rampant deforestation, eroding soils, spreading deserts, loss of biological diversity, the destruction of fisheries, and polluted and degraded urban environments threaten to spread environmental impoverishment, particularly in the tropics, where human population growth is greatest.

It is important to recognize that environmental degradation and human poverty are closely linked. Impoverished people desperate for land on which to grow crops or graze cattle are destroying forests and overgrazing even more marginal land. These people become trapped in a vicious downward spiral. They have little choice but to continue to overexploit the weakened resources available to them. Continued abuse of these lands only diminishes their productivity. Throughout the developing world, alarming amounts of land rendered useless by over-grazing and poor agricultural practices have become virtual wastelands, yet human numbers continue to multiply in these areas.

From Bangladesh to Haiti, we are confronted with an increasing number of ecological basket cases. In the Philippines, a traditional focus of U.S. interest, environmental devastation is widespread as deforestation, soil erosion, and the destruction of coral reefs and fisheries combine with the highest population growth rate in Southeast Asia.

Controlling human population growth is the key factor in the environmental equation. World population is expected to at least double to about 11 billion before leveling off. Most of this growth will occur in the poorest nations of the developing world. I would hope that the United States will once again become a strong advocate of international efforts to promote family planning. Bringing human populations into a sustainable balance with their natural resource base must be a vital objective of U.S. foreign policy.

Foreign economic assistance, the program of the Agency for International Development (AID), can become a potentially powerful tool for arresting environmental deterioration in developing countries. People who profess to care about global environmental problems— the loss of biological diversity, the destruction of tropical forests, the greenhouse effect, the impoverishment of the marine environment, and so on—should be strong supporters of foreign aid planning and the principles of sustainable development urged by the World Commission on Environment and Development, the "Brundtland Commission."

If sustainability is to be the underlying element of overseas assistance programs, so too must it be a guiding principle in people's practices at home. Too often we think of sustainable development only in terms of the resources of other countries. We have much that we can and should be doing to promote long-term sustainability in our own resource management. The conflict over our own rainforests, the old growth forests of the Pacific Northwest, illustrates this point.

The decade ahead will be a time of great activity on the environmental front, both globally and domestically. I sincerely believe we will be tested as we have been only in times of war and during the Great Depression. We must set goals for the year 2000 that will challenge both the American people and the world community.

Despite the complexities ahead, I remain an optimist. I am confident that if we collectively commit ourselves to a clean, healthy environment we can surpass the achievements of the 1980s and meet the serious challenges that face us in the coming decades. I hope that today's students will recognize their significant role in and responsibility for bringing about change and will rise to the occasion to improve the quality of our global environment.

A sunset in Appalachia takes on a grim aspect thanks to the destruction wrought there by acid rain.

c h a p t e r   1

K I L L E R   R A I N

Adirondack Park is the largest national park in the country. At 6 million acres it is 3 times the size of Yellowstone and bigger than the state of Massachusetts. It is also one of the most beautiful regions in the United States. Covering nearly 10,000 square miles, its 4,000-foot mountains—remains of an ancient chain that once soared as high as the Himalayas—are blanketed in evergreen and deciduous forests, tumbling brooks and waterfalls, and placid lakes. Much of it is untrod wilderness, with only a handful of intrepid hikers penetrating its farthest reaches every year.

One would think this haven of nature was secure from danger. Yet there is hardly a place in the United States that is suffering under as great a threat to its wildlife and very existence as is Adirondack Park. Scores of its lakes are now unable to support fish life. Trees, especially those nearest mountaintops, are dying by the thousands. Soil, which in these granite mountains is but a thin skin over a rocky skeleton, is being contaminated. Even the drinking water of the people who live there is threatened.

The threat comes from the sky—in rain. It is one of the tragic ironies of the modern world that rain, which has nourished all life on earth for eons, should now carry the means to destroy that life. Yet it does, in the form of pollution spewed from millions of factory chimneys, house furnaces, and car tail pipes around the world. These emitters release substances that turn into acids in the atmosphere and then return to earth when it rains.

When it comes to *acid rain*, as this killing rainfall is popularly known, Adirondack Park has everything going against it. It is directly downwind of this country's industrial heartland, centered in the Ohio Valley. Its clear lakes and thin soils are poorly equipped to neutralize acids—that is, to render them harmless. The region is high in altitude, meaning not only are trees more likely to be bathed in acidic fogs and mists than trees at lower altitudes, but they have to deal with more stress from wind and cold. As a result, they are more vulnerable to added pressure from acid rain.

The Adirondacks are not the only victim. Killer rain is falling all over the country—indeed, the world. In the United States, the Northeast is the worst-hit region. But other areas are also at risk: the Southeast, the Great Lakes region, the West Coast, even the Rocky Mountains. And the prevailing west-to-east winds that blow the bulk of the middle western states' industrial pollution into the Adirondacks continue to blow it right into eastern Canada. There the soils are just as thin, the lakes as much at risk. In fact, thousands of lakes—not hundreds, as in the Adirondacks—are dead, dying, or in grave danger.

Other countries are suffering as badly or worse from acid rain. In Europe, 50 million hectares of forests have been damaged

Acid rain has caused extensive tree damage in the United States—particularly in eastern states—as well as around the world.

by acid rain, according to the Worldwatch Institute, a figure that represents 35% of Europe's total woodlands. (One hectare equals approximately 2.5 acres, or an area slightly larger than 2 football fields.) In Sweden, where experts first documented acid rain's lethal effects on fish and other marine life—and where prevailing winds blow thousands of tons of central and Eastern Europe's pollution each year—14,000 lakes are unable to support sensitive aquatic life. Eastern Europe and the Soviet Union, where pollution controls have been much more lax than in Western countries, have suffered even worse environmental degradation. Acid rain is also a growing problem in Third World countries—such as China and India, the world's two most populous nations—where energy demands are increasing and pollution controls are all but nonexistent.

BIRTH OF ACID RAIN

People have been aware of air pollution ever since the philosopher Seneca remarked on Rome's polluted skies in A.D. 61. Yet throughout history, even after the Industrial Revolution, which started in the 18th century and serves as the official beginning of serious regional and global air pollution, human beings have notoriously ignored the problem. Acid rain—air pollution's most dangerous manifestation—is no exception.

An Englishman named Charles Angus Smith can be called the father of acid rain research, for he first suggested, in 1852, that sulfuric acid in Manchester, England, was causing metal to rust and dyed goods to fade in this industrial city. Yet his work, and the efforts of others who tried to sound the alarm about this airborne pollution over the ensuing decades, went unnoticed. Then, in December 1952—exactly 100 years after Smith's initial declaration—what newspapers often called the "black fog" descended on London for several days. Freak weather patterns held all the pollution rising from London's chimneys within a few hundred feet of the ground; it was as if a giant lid had been placed over the city. Before it lifted on December 7, the fog had killed 4,000 Londoners and left tens of thousands ill.

Even after such a tragedy, experts and laypeople alike remained largely unconcerned. Only a few solitary scientists working in widely scattered parts of the world began to understand the potentially devastating effects of air pollution and acid rain. In the 1950s they began to find hard data.

Why did it take almost 200 years after the advent of the Industrial Revolution for the full impact of acid rain to be noticed? The answer has to do largely with population. In general, the more people on earth, the more pollution is generated. Acid rain increased in tandem with the growth of the world's population, which expanded from 725 million in 1750 to 1.6 billion in 1900 to 2.5 billion in 1950. Although slow to become evident, acid rain's effects came to the fore about this time because the amount of air pollution spewed into world skies—and later falling as acid rain—had reached staggering proportions.

During the 1950s a young Canadian ecologist named Eville Gorham began publishing a series of papers in which he held that acid precipitation could affect the *buffering*, or neutralizing, capacity of lakes, soils, and bedrock. Gorham and his colleague F. J. H. Mackereth, working in England's Lake District—a landscape similar in many ways to the Adirondacks—discovered a number of acidified tarns (small, steep-banked mountain lakes fed by rainwater). The two scientists asserted that the acidification of these waters was caused by air pollution.

Yet even warnings by respected researchers such as Gorham and Mackereth were largely ignored. It was not until the late 1960s that a Swedish researcher, Dr. Svante Odén, helped make acid rain a household term. Odén, who theorized that pollution blowing into Sweden from other countries was the cause of increasingly acidic Swedish waters, published his findings first in a Swedish newspaper, then in a respected scientific journal.

Odén demonstrated for the first time that rain and surface water throughout Europe were becoming more acidic and that winds were fanning sulfur- and nitrogen-based pollutants across the continent. Odén's findings, which also revealed how acid rain could cause declines in fish populations, reduced forest growth, and disintegration of materials, "led to a veritable storm of scientific and public concern about acid precipitation," wrote Dr. Ellis Cowling of North Carolina State's School of Forest Resources.

Thus, acid rain as a worldwide threat was born. Later, the U.S. Acid Precipitation Act of 1980 led Cowling and others to

Emissions from fossil-fuel burning can cause deadly smogs, such as the one that settled over London, England, in December 1952, killing thousands.

develop the National Acid Precipitation Assessment Program (NAPAP), a 10-year government study of pollution falling at a series of atmospheric sampling stations across the country. Other nations have followed suit, and acid rain and its environmental effects are now monitored throughout the world.

WHAT IS ACID RAIN?

Acid rain is the popular term for this widespread phenomenon and will be used throughout this book. But scientists prefer the term *acid deposition* because once in the air, acidic pollution can be deposited—that is, reach the ground—not just in rain but in snow, hail, sleet, fog, mist, dew, and even attached to dry particles that simply drop out of the sky by the force of gravity.

Acid rain forms in the atmosphere from chemical substances created by the burning of fossil fuels. When coal and oil are ignited, they release sulfur and nitrogen oxide gases, the precursors of acid rain. These gases include sulfur dioxide (SO_2) and several oxides of nitrogen, including nitric oxide (NO) and nitrogen dioxide (NO_2), collectively designated by the symbol NO_x. Though invisible, sulfur dioxide and nitrogen oxides rise with the black, sooty smoke that sometimes pours from factory chimneys or in the white exhaust that can be seen billowing from car tail pipes on cold days.

Once released into the atmosphere, sulfur dioxide and nitrogen oxides react with other airborne chemicals, water vapor, and sunlight to produce sulfuric and nitric acids—the acids in acid rain. Atmospheric chemists still do not fully understand how these highly complex chemical reactions take place or what role temperature, wind, sunlight, and other climatic factors play. But although the causes may be hard to decipher, the effects are not. The old adage "What goes up must come down" is all too true. Often these pollutants do not come down right away, however. In fact, they can reside in the atmosphere for several days, where strong winds transport them sometimes hundreds or even thousands of miles before precipitation carries them back to earth. During this time, they turn into harmful acids.

THE pH SCALE

Chemists determine how acidic a substance is by using what is called the pH scale. Literally "potential of hydrogen," pH measures acidity—and alkalinity, its opposite—on a 14-point scale. Anything higher than 7 on this scale is alkaline; anything

One of the main culprits in the acid rain story is the automobile, which emits nitrogen oxide exhausts that react in the air to form harmful acids.

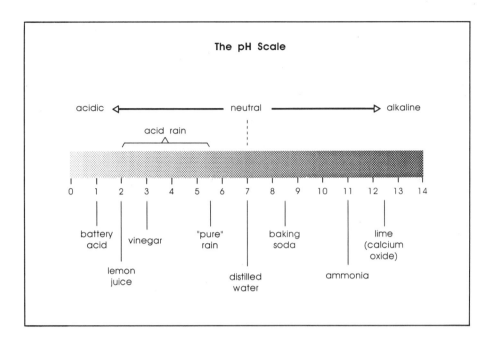

The pH Scale

acidic ←——————————— neutral ——————————→ alkaline

acid rain

0 1 2 3 4 5 6 7 8 9 10 11 12 13 14

battery acid · vinegar · "pure" rain · baking soda · lime (calcium oxide)

lemon juice · distilled water · ammonia

below, acidic. The ratio of positively charged hydrogen ions to negatively charged hydroxyl ions in a particular substance determines its pH. (An ion is any electrically charged particle.) A substance that contains equal amounts of hydrogen and hydroxyl ions has a pH of 7, or neutral. The greater the ratio of hydrogen ions to hydroxyl ions in a substance, the more acidic it is, and the lower its pH. .

The pH scale is logarithmic, so that each whole number on the scale represents a tenfold increase or decrease. For example, battery acid, with a pH of 1, is 10 times more acidic than lemon juice, with a pH of 2, 100 times more acidic than vinegar (pH 3), and 10,000,000 times more acidic than baking soda (pH 8).

Clean rain is generally slightly acidic (pH 5.6) because a weak carbonic acid forms naturally in the earth's carbon-rich atmosphere. But rain falling on the Adirondacks and other parts of the Northeast is often more than 100 times more acidic. The U.S. Environmental Protection Agency (EPA) estimates that rainfall over the eastern part of North America now averages approximately pH 4.5, or about as acidic as tomato juice. By contrast, ice cores taken from glaciers in Greenland reveal that snow that fell about 200 years ago averaged about neutral (pH 7), which clearly shows how much humans have acidified the atmosphere since the dawn of the Industrial Revolution. The lowest pH level ever recorded fell on Wheeling, West Virginia. It registered a pH of 2.2—only slightly less acidic than lemon juice.

ACID RAIN TODAY

Throughout the world, acid rain continues to escalate, threatening trees, crops, lakes, streams, drinking-water supplies, buildings, bridges, ancient monuments, and animal life, from the tiniest insect right up through fish and birds to the world's top predator: man. In many countries, particularly in the Third World, the problem is only going to get worse as rapidly expanding populations burn more and more fossil fuels to heat their homes, cook their food, and power their smoke-belching cars, motorbikes, and buses.

Yet there is hope. In the United States, the highest per capita energy user in the world, President George Bush signed a revised Clean Air Act into law in November 1990 that he called "the most significant air pollution legislation in our nation's history." At annual costs of up to $25 billion, the new regulations call for industry to cut sulfur dioxide emissions by 10 million tons per year (a halving of 1980 levels) and nitrogen oxides by 2 million tons per year, among other pollution-reducing measures that will be in effect by the end of the decade.

Europe, the world's second biggest polluter after the United States, has also called for sweeping changes. Under the auspices of the United Nations Economic Commission for Europe (ECE), many European countries have agreed to slash sulfur dioxide emissions by 30% from 1980 levels by 1993 and to impose a freeze on nitrogen oxide emissions in 1994 at 1987 levels, with further discussions in 1996 aimed at actual reductions. In Eastern European nations and the Soviet Union, political changes now under way may enable these countries to better curb the massive amounts of pollution emitted each year that are killing trees, fish, and perhaps even people in their own and neighboring lands.

In coming decades, poor and underdeveloped Third World nations will become the worst polluters. Yet with financial and technological help from developed nations, the Third World may also begin to slow dangerous emissions. Perhaps the greatest hope of all is that environmental awareness—concern for the well-being of our planet—has reached heights never before seen, not only in this country but around the world. If this concern keeps up and is backed by cooperative international action, the earth's rain may yet return to its natural purity.

Once a symbol of industrial progress, smokestacks now also call to mind a less uplifting concept—air pollution.

V I C I O U S   C Y C L E

The vicious cycle of acid rain began hundreds of millions of years ago. For it was over countless eons that fuel products such as coal, oil, and natural gas, which are burned for power and which ultimately cause acid rain, formed deep beneath the earth's surface.

Amazing as it may sound, coal and petroleum are born of the remains of living things in an extremely slow process that works as follows: Throughout their lives, all plants and animals, including human beings, absorb carbon. In a process known as photosynthesis, plants absorb carbon dioxide from the atmosphere, using the carbon to grow. Animals assimilate carbon when they feed upon plants. When these flora and fauna die and decompose, the carbon stored within their tissues disintegrates at a more or less steady rate and returns to the atmosphere as gaseous carbon dioxide. However, if those organic remains do not decompose fully, they can—in time and under the proper conditions—turn into coal, oil, and other so-called *fossil fuels*.

Coal has its roots in the Carboniferous period, 345 to 280 million years ago. During that geologic period, vast stands of trees, shrubs, and other vegetation grew in swamps, peat bogs, and other low-lying wetlands around the world. When these plants—and the animals that lived among them—died, their remains settled into the ground. There they only partially decomposed before accumulating layers of sediment and rock transformed them, over millions of years, into seams of coal.

Coal, then, is composed largely of carbon, with varying amounts of mineral matter. Anthracite, or hard coal, is the highest quality coal; peat, the lowest quality. Major coal fields in the United States are found in Appalachia, the Midwest, the Rocky Mountains, and the Gulf Coast. Europe's largest coal-producing nations are Germany, Great Britain, Poland, France, and Belgium. The Soviet Union, China, India, South Africa, and Australia also have huge reserves.

Like coal, petroleum (also called crude oil) is formed from the incompletely decomposed remains of plants and animals. High temperatures and pressures exerted by over-lying rock transform the organic matter in these remains into *hydrocarbons*, which are organic compounds that contain only hydrogen and carbon. At a refinery, crude oil is separated into a range of fuel substances, including natural gas, gasoline, kero-sene, diesel fuel, heating oils, and tars. In 1980, the leading oil producers were the Soviet Union, Saudi Arabia, the United States, Iraq, Venezuela, China, Nigeria, Mexico, Libya, and the United Arab Emirates. The world's biggest reserves lie in the Middle East.

Natural gas, or methane, is formed under the same geologic conditions as oil and often overlays oil fields. Natural gas is actually the most volatile form of petroleum, yet unlike crude oil, it may contain components produced from inorganic processes, such as volcanic activity. The United States and the

Soviet Union are the biggest producers of natural gas, which
supplies about one-fifth of the energy generated by fossil fuels.

BURNING FOSSILS

When fossil fuels are burned, not only is carbon
released—in the form of carbon dioxide, a so-called greenhouse
gas that traps heat within the earth's atmosphere and has been
implicated in the supposed global warming now taking
place—but so are any other chemical impurities that happen to
be within that fossil fuel. These include sulfur, nitrogen, and
various trace metals, including arsenic, mercury, aluminum, and
nearly 50 others.

*Large reserves of coal in the United States and many other countries
make this fossil fuel a likely source of electric power for years to come.*

In terms of acid rain, sulfur and nitrogen are the two most insidious chemical "extras" within fossil fuels. Depending on the amount of sulfur, which ranges from less than 1% to as much as 6%, coal is often labeled as high sulfur, medium sulfur, or low sulfur. Burning a ton of high-sulfur coal may release as much as 120 pounds of sulfur. By contrast, natural gas has little sulfur, but large quantities of nitrogen. In essence, the amount of pollutants emitted depends on the sulfur and nitrogen content of the fossil fuel, and for nitrogen, on the temperature and efficiency of combustion.

When incinerated, solid sulfur turns into gaseous sulfur dioxide, whereas solid nitrogen becomes various gaseous oxides of nitrogen. Sulfur and nitrogen oxides fly up factory smokestacks and out of car tail pipes into the atmosphere, where, under the proper conditions, they further oxidize into sulfuric and nitric acids. Rain and other processes then carry these acids to the ground.

Fossil fuels are burned to power electric power plants, industrial boilers, smelters, businesses, schools, homes, and vehicles of all sorts, from jetliners to the family car. In 1985, these various energy sources contributed 23.1 million tons of sulfur dioxide and 20.5 million tons of nitrogen oxides to U.S. skies. Worldwide, according to the Worldwatch Institute, the atmosphere receives about as much sulfur from human activities as it does naturally—about 75 to 100 million tons per year. (Sulfur is released naturally by oceanic plankton, swamps and other wetlands, and erupting volcanoes.) Yet most emissions occur on just 5% of the land surface, primarily in eastern North America, Europe, and China. That is why acid rain is so threatening—it is concentrated.

ELECTRIC FACTORY

On the banks of the Ohio River near Cheshire, Ohio, sits the General James M. Gavin electric power plant. Owned and operated by American Electric Power Corporation, the largest for-profit electric company in the world, Gavin generates enough electricity to supply the energy needs of 600,000 Ohio residents.

A lot of coal is burned to create that energy—7.5 million tons per year. Each hour on the average, 860 tons of coal are delivered by barge and conveyer belt from nearby coal mines operated by the parent company exclusively to feed Gavin's two 25-story-tall boilers.

Inside the plant—as inside almost any other coal-fired electric factory—coal is first crushed by giant, hardened-steel pulverizers, then washed to remove impurities that might reduce combustion efficiency. (Gavin's coal contains 3.7% sulfur, but only 0.2% is taken out at this stage.) Giant fans then blow coal dust and air into the 2 boilers, where they burst into flame at roughly 3,500 degrees Fahrenheit. Purified water within tubes in the boiler instantly becomes superheated steam that then hits turbines at a pressure of 3,500 pounds per square inch. The turbines, in turn, cause huge magnets to rotate within copper coils, which push the electrons that later light the lamps and power the refrigerators of Gavin's customers.

That is the good part of electric power generation. The bad part comes next. Along with sulfur and nitrogen, hydrogen, oxygen, and trace metals that can be separated from the coal only by burning are released. These gases charge up Gavin's smokestack at speeds of up to 55 miles per hour and at temperatures as high as 700°F. Until this stage, the chemicals that cause acid rain

A research helicopter equipped to measure trace metals, gases, and other emissions hovers above a coal-fired power plant in Colstrip, Montana.

have been bound harmlessly within organic remains for millions of years. Suddenly they break free, ready to cause damage to living and nonliving things for hundreds or thousands of miles around.

TALL-STACK FALLACY

In the late 1960s, environmentalists took great pains to convince industry that its pollution was causing grave ecological and structural damage. They pointed to the landscape around coal-fired plants, which often displayed dead and dying trees, blackened buildings, and ruined crops. Industry executives took notice and offered what they considered the perfect solution: tall smokestacks.

In 1950, the average smokestack height in the Ohio Valley was 320 feet; by 1980, that average had more than doubled to 740 feet. Gavin's stack is one of the highest in the United States: 1,103 feet. The granddaddy of them all is in

Canada at INCO, a copper-nickel smelter outside Sudbury, Ontario. Its "superstack" is 1,250 feet high.

Soaring chimneys, industry argued, would carry gaseous emissions high into the atmosphere, to be dispersed harmlessly. These emissions do not simply vanish, however, and eventually they return to the earth. Chemicals such as carbon dioxide and methane may stay in the atmosphere for up to 100 years, which is why they are dangerous as greenhouse gases that contribute to global warming. Sulfur and nitrogen oxides remain aloft only for several days.

As it turns out, the tall stacks actually increased the likelihood of acid rain. When emitted from the older, shorter stacks, pollutants fell to the ground sooner and closer to the factory. When emitted from stacks hundreds of feet taller, they were carried high into the atmosphere, often to twice the height of the stack. Spending more time in the air, the sulfur and nitrogen oxides had a greater chance of oxidizing into sulfuric and nitric acids, acid rain's lethal weapons.

The problem went even further. Giant chimneys spewed pollutants high enough to be picked up by the *jet stream*, the high-altitude system of winds that flows around the planet Earth at speeds often exceeding 240 miles per hour. Once in the jet stream, which generally flows west to east across North America, the chemicals were carried hundreds or even thousands of miles before returning to earth. Despite good intentions, the electric establishment was not only sending its pollution elsewhere but also giving it plenty of time—as long as five days—to fall into the wrong chemical crowd and turn acidic.

There is another problem with such long-distance travel. Air pollution does not respect boundaries. It crosses state lines and international borders with impunity. Thus, the Ohio River valley's pollution, hitching a ride on the jet stream, sweeps through the eastern Atlantic states into New England and beyond, into eastern Canada, before finally blowing out into the Atlantic Ocean.

Naturally, New York State is not too happy that pollution from Ohio, Illinois, and other midwestern states ends up in the state's prized Adirondack Park. Nor for that matter is Canada, which has determined that 60% of the sulfur landing in its eastern provinces originates in the United States. In fact, U.S.-Canadian relations have reached their lowest point in decades in the dispute over this pollution.

The so-called transboundary problem is not restricted to North America. Prevailing winds blow much of central Europe's pollution north into Scandinavia. According to the Worldwatch Institute, 96% of the 210,000 tons of sulfur pollution that fell on Norway in 1988 originated in other countries. For Sweden— as well as for Austria and Switzerland at the other end of Europe —the figure was about 90%. Much of this pollution comes down as acid rain.

What can states and nations do about this undeclared state of chemical warfare? Because governments cannot control the weather and winds blow where they will, the only way to slow the pollutants imported into a region is to curb their exportation from originating regions. And since reining in air pollution once it is in the air is clearly impossible, the best way to slow the exportation of pollutants is to slow their creation. Thus, national and international agreements to slash emissions at the source remain the only viable solution (see Chapter 7).

Electric power plants such as Gavin are not the only source of sulfur and nitrogen oxides. Fossil fuels also run industrial boilers and refineries. They heat public buildings and private businesses, schools and houses. And they power mechanical devices of all kinds, from Chevrolets to chain saws. Finally, *smelting*—the process of separating a metal from its ore—also causes the release of sulfur, because lead, zinc, nickel, and copper often come from sulfur-bearing rock.

Nevertheless, electric power plants, which run 24 hours a day nationwide, produce by far the largest amount of sulfur

Rising 1,250 feet in the sky, the "superstack" at the INCO smelter in Ontario, Canada, is the tallest in the world. Tall smokestacks send pollutants higher into the atmosphere, causing them to travel farther from their source.

Nitrogen oxide emissions have been on the rise in recent years because of the burgeoning number of buses and other vehicles on the roads.

pollution in the United States. According to a 1980 report by Environment Canada, the environmental arm of the Canadian government, coal- and oil-fired power plants generated fully two-thirds of the sulfur dioxide released in the United States. Industrial boilers, smelters, and refineries contributed 28%, and transportation and commercial institutions and homes added just 3% each.

   Yet while electric power plants are this country's biggest sulfur dioxide polluters, the picture is nearly reversed when talking of nitrogen oxide pollution. In the United States, the report found, 44% of nitrogen oxides came from transportation sources. That category includes cars, buses, motorcycles, trucks, ships, airplanes, diesel-powered trains, and any other form of transportation that burns fossil fuels. The remainder of U.S. nitrogen oxides came from power plants (29%), industrial sources (23%), and commercial institutions and homes (4%). In Canada, transportation accounts for an even greater slice of that country's nitrogen oxide pie: 61%.

Because engines of cars and other vehicles are the largest nitrogen oxide polluters, it is useful to know how they operate. Although the parts are different, the process is not far removed from that of a power plant such as Gavin. In this country, the typical car has a four-stroke internal-combustion engine. The first stroke sucks in a mixture of gas and air. The second compresses it. The third ignites the mixture—at about 4,500°F—and transmits the power to the wheels via the axles. The fourth stroke vents burned gas to the atmosphere through the exhaust pipe. What is released is a blend of nitrogen oxides, hydrocarbons, and carbon monoxide, all of which are highly poisonous to breathe. Nitrogen oxides can also create more long term and widespread hazards, including ground-level ozone, or smog, and acid rain.

In fact, nitrogen oxides are of more concern to environmentalists and others worried about acid rain in this country than is sulfur dioxide. According to the EPA, between 1970 and 1987 the United States cut sulfur dioxide emissions by 28%, mostly because of new controls imposed by the 1970 Clean Air Act and energy efficiency brought on by the mid-1970s energy crisis.

By contrast, emissions of nitrogen oxides have steadily risen. Since the 1950s, nitrogen oxide emissions have doubled in the United States and tripled in Canada. Since 1980, nitrogen oxide releases in North America have begun to level off, but the sheer number of new cars on the road every year keeps the level of nitrogen oxides high. Yet while the U.S. and Canadian governments insist on mandatory catalytic converters (devices that produce cleaner exhaust) and other antipollution measures, many other countries, particularly in the Third World, do not. With diesel-powered vehicles lacking even the simplest pollution controls and millions of motorbikes with their highly polluting two-stroke engines, these nations—and their neighbors—have a lot to worry about down the road when it comes to acid rain.

AIRBORNE ACIDS

Once sulfur and nitrogen oxides are released into the atmosphere, these colorless, odorless gases react with water vapor, carbon dioxide, sunlight, ozone, hydrocarbons, methane, and other atmospheric substances to become acids.

The scenario is played out in the troposphere (the lower seven miles of the atmosphere) and a whole series of chemical reactions must take place before the stage is set for acid rain's debut. The process begins when sunlight strikes and splits apart a molecule of ozone (O_3), which is produced either near the ground by nitrogen oxides or high in the ozone layer. The result is a molecule of oxygen (O_2) and an atom of oxygen (O). The oxygen atom is highly reactive and soon combines with a water molecule (H_2O) to form two hydroxyl radicals (HO). This is a rare but active species of bonded atoms that—in processes still not completely understood by chemists—transforms nitrogen oxides into nitric acid (HNO_3) and initiates the reactions that turn sulfur dioxide into sulfuric acid (H_2SO_4). These acidic substances are readily absorbed by cloud droplets that, when heavy enough, fall to earth as acid rain.

From the compaction of fossil fuels over millions of years to the moment an acidic drop lands on a leaf, lake, or building, the life cyle of acid rain is a long, involved process. But once unleashed, the scourge of acid rain takes just the blink of an eye, comparatively speaking, to wreak havoc on plants, animals, ecosystems, artifacts, and, most scary of all, humans.

The corrosion of features on this statue outside the Field Museum of Natural History in Chicago is probably caused by acid rain.

chapter 3

A C I D   B A T H

It is a tragic twist of fate that the fossilized remains of
ancient plants and animals should endanger their modern-day
descendants. But the acid rain unleashed when humans burn
fossil fuels now seriously threatens trees, crops, insects, crustaceans, fish, birds, and other wildlife. It threatens the ecosystems,
such as soils, ponds, and forests, in which these plants and
animals live. And it threatens nonliving things, including buildings, ancient stone monuments, water-supply pipes, and
underground aquifers (water-bearing layers of rock). Most
significantly, it threatens men, women, and children.

It should be noted that no discussion of the impact of
acid rain can ignore its forerunners, sulfur and nitrogen oxides,
and its fellow pollutant ozone (also formed from nitrogen oxides,
although in a different manner than acid rain). In fact, many
researchers believe that the effects of acid rain are worsened by
those of ozone and other forms of air pollution.

Acid rain does not kill trees outright but weakens them to the point where they become susceptible to extremes of heat or cold, attacks from blight-causing viruses or from insects such as the gypsy moth, and other environmental stresses.

Some researchers believe that a whole host of stresses must work in concert to bring down a tree. Dr. Gene Likens of the New York Botanical Gardens has studied the effects of acids at the Hubbard Brook Experimental Forest in New Hampshire since 1963, the longest record of precipitation chemistry in North America. In a 1989 issue of the scientific journal *Ambio*, Likens wrote that "the combined effects of drought, an excessively cold autumn or winter, plus acid cloud water, plus high ozone concentrations, plus an outbreak of herbivorous [plant-eating] insects, etc. could initiate forest decline, while each (or a few) of these stresses acting alone may not produce a serious effect."

How does acid rain stress a tree? For one thing, it can make conifers (an order of cone-bearing, usually evergreen, trees and bushes) more susceptible to cold, according to preliminary findings by scientists at the Boyce Thompson Institute in Ithaca, New York. In the fall, conifers such as red spruce—perhaps the species most stressed by acid rain—normally prepare for the freezing temperatures of winter by withdrawing water from their needles. Tree roots initiate this undertaking, known as *cold hardening*, by slowing the release of nitrogen-bearing nutrients from the soil. Nitrogen-rich acids soaking into needles might override that signal from the roots, causing cold hardening to be delayed and leaving a tree vulnerable to freezing of needle

The combined effects of acid rain and ozone appear to have taken a toll on the spruce and fir trees atop North Carolina's Mount Mitchell.

tissues. Ozone, too, might lower a tree's resistance to freezing by damaging cell membranes.

Many scientists, in fact, believe that acid rain often works in conjunction with ozone to stress a tree. Not only can ozone damage chlorophyll, thereby slowing photosynthesis and tree growth, but it can also damage the water-resistant waxy coating of needles. This coating not only retards water loss from the tree but keeps harmful substances out and helps in the exchange of gases. Once this coating is removed, acids can penetrate needles, where they can disrupt the tree's cold-hardening strategy and also leach vital nutrients, such as magnesium, potassium, and calcium, from the tree. Scientist Robert Bruck and his colleagues at North Carolina State University discovered that rainwater dripping from leaves contained far more magnesium, sodium, potassium, and calcium than rainfall that missed the trees.

Not only do trees suffer from acids attacking leaves or needles aboveground and fine roots belowground, but they also appear to produce their own acids. Scientists at the University of Göttingen's Institute for Soil Sciences and Forest Nutrition in Germany found that trees' foliage and bark oxidize sulfur dioxide from the atmosphere into sulfuric acid. As a result, water washed to the forest floor is between two and four times as acidic—depending on the types of trees—as the original rain hitting the forest canopy, or topmost layer of branches.

IN THE CLOUDS

Trees at high altitudes face even more trouble from acid rain and ozone. In fact, most of the damage to U.S. forests has been in high-altitude regions, such as the Adirondack and Appalachian mountains.

Why do trees high up face a graver risk? Often standing directly downwind of pollution sources, they frequently get the most potent dose of pollution, and being high up, they grow in landscapes first struck when acid rain falls. Furthermore, at such elevations trees are already more stressed by wind and cold than their neighbors at lower altitudes. Most critical, they are often wrapped for long periods in clouds and mist, up to 3,000 hours each year. Not only can clouds and mist contain just as much acid as can rain, but that acidity filters down to the base of clouds, which are often the parts touching mountains—and their mantle of forests.

North Carolina's Mount Mitchell is a case in point. At 6,684 feet, it is the highest mountain in eastern North America. Its slopes are covered in red spruce and Fraser fir—the very types of

trees that are exhibiting reduced growth and general decline
straight up the Appalachians and into eastern Canada as well as
throughout the forests of Europe. Clouds typically bathe the top
of Mount Mitchell 8 out of every 10 days.

In studies over several years in the early 1980s, North
Carolina State's Robert Bruck found that about half of the time,
ozone levels on the summit exceeded the amount proven to
cause damage to trees in controlled laboratory experiments.
Levels of ozone sometimes increased to twice the minimum
needed to injure a tree. Acid levels were also extraordinarily
high, ranging from pH 2.12 to pH 2.9. That is, precipitation on
the mountain averages about 1,000 times more acidic than if it
were falling through a pristine atmosphere.

*High-altitude forests undergo added stress from being frequently bathed
in acidic clouds and mists.*

Photographs taken of Mount Mitchell show hundreds of dead or damaged trees extending far down the flanks of the mountain, right down to the level where hardwoods take over from evergreens. Similar photographs can be seen of mountainsides in the Adirondacks, in the Poconos of Pennsylvania, in New Hampshire's White Mountains and Vermont's Green Mountains, in eastern Canada, in Germany's Bavaria, in Poland and other Eastern European countries, and in parts of southwestern China. And these are just the hardest-hit areas. What other forests are suffering undue stress? Will they soon go the way of these token dead and dying stands?

"It's plain that no one has proved, or ever will, that air pollution is killing the trees up here," Bruck told an *Audubon* reporter of Mount Mitchell's plight. "But far more quickly than we ever expected, we've ended up with a highly correlated bunch of data—high levels of air pollution correlated to a decline we're watching in progress."

Acid rain's consequences may be difficult to prove in the field, where countless environmental factors must be considered. But in controlled laboratory tests, effects can be pinpointed with greater accuracy. In an experiment at North Carolina's Coweeta Hydrologic Laboratory, 3 University of Georgia researchers gave an acid bath—with pHs ranging from 2.5 to 0.5—to 8 different plant species, including red maple, flowering dogwood, and other flora typical of the mountains of which Mount Mitchell is the centerpiece. According to the researchers, results suggest that "a tenfold increase in acidity from pH 3.2 to 2.2 in a single spring or summer storm could bring damage or death to mature leaves of dominant flowering plants in the southern Appalachians."

Ecosystems at high latitudes may suffer for essentially the same reasons as those at high altitudes. In the regions that cover the arctic belt that girdles the globe in northern parts of Alaska, Canada, Scandinavia, and the Soviet Union, plants and animals are highly stressed by low temperatures and seasonal light that, above the Arctic Circle, means total darkness for up to three months each year.

Contrary to what one might think, the Arctic and Antarctic are not so far removed from industrialized regions of the world as to be safe from air pollution. Dr. Daniel Jaffe of the University of Alaska at Fairbanks (UAF) and others have found traces of sulfate and nitrate on Alaska's remote North Slope, more than 100 miles north of the Arctic Circle. (Sulfate and nitrate are the constituents, with hydrogen, of sulfuric and nitric acids,

' They believe this pollution is carried by the jet

~~ and the Soviet Union.

f these pollutants are

. As James MacKenzie

Resources Institute wrote

ril 1989), "If it turns out

ıd to significant nutrient

ılt over a long period as

period."

ready occurred. Near Norilsk,

ıad to completely change their

ipal food, has suffered poorly

White of UAF's Institute of

A researcher analyzes lichen, a plant very susceptible to acid rain damage.

Arctic Biology. In this heavily polluted Siberian region, which is downwind of major Soviet factories, lichen growth has dropped to just 1% to 2% of normal levels, and the number of lichen species has plummeted from about 50 to perhaps 3 or 4, says White.

CROPS

Acid rain's effects on crops are still little understood. But again, many researchers feel that acid rain can work in league with other pollutants. Says leading acid rain researcher Ellis Cowling, "Sulfur dioxide, ozone, oxides of nitrogen, fluoride, and

Ecosystems at high latitudes may suffer for essentially the same reasons as those at high altitudes. In the regions that cover the arctic belt that girdles the globe in northern parts of Alaska, Canada, Scandinavia, and the Soviet Union, plants and animals are highly stressed by low temperatures and seasonal light that, above the Arctic Circle, means total darkness for up to three months each year.

Contrary to what one might think, the Arctic and Antarctic are not so far removed from industrialized regions of the world as to be safe from air pollution. Dr. Daniel Jaffe of the University of Alaska at Fairbanks (UAF) and others have found traces of sulfate and nitrate on Alaska's remote North Slope, more than 100 miles north of the Arctic Circle. (Sulfate and nitrate are the constituents, with hydrogen, of sulfuric and nitric acids, respectively.) They believe this pollution is carried by the jet stream from factories in Europe and the Soviet Union.

Even though the concentrations of these pollutants are minute, they could have serious impacts. As James MacKenzie and Mohamed T. El-Ashry of the World Resources Institute wrote in an article in *Technology Review* (April 1989), "If it turns out that lower levels of acid deposition lead to significant nutrient leaching, the same injuries could result over a long period as result from higher levels over a short period."

In fact, serious injury has already occurred. Near Norilsk, in northern Siberia, reindeer have had to completely change their habitat because lichen, their principal food, has suffered poorly from acid rain, reports Dr. Robert White of UAF's Institute of

A researcher analyzes lichen, a plant very susceptible to acid rain damage.

Arctic Biology. In this heavily polluted Siberian region, which is downwind of major Soviet factories, lichen growth has dropped to just 1% to 2% of normal levels, and the number of lichen species has plummeted from about 50 to perhaps 3 or 4, says White.

CROPS

Acid rain's effects on crops are still little understood. But again, many researchers feel that acid rain can work in league with other pollutants. Says leading acid rain researcher Ellis Cowling, "Sulfur dioxide, ozone, oxides of nitrogen, fluoride, and hydrogen chloride cause serious damage to crops that must be considered together with the possible effects of acid deposition."

Simulated experiments in the field, laboratory, and greenhouse have shown that acid rain predisposes plants to infection by bacteria or viruses and lowers their resistance to insect attacks. Acids also speed the erosion of leaf-surface wax—which has the same protective properties for plants as it does for trees—and induce lesions on foliage. Finally, acid rain may inhibit nitrogen fixation by bacteria, a process in which soil bacteria absorb atmospheric nitrogen that, when the bacteria die, fertilizes, or enriches, the soil.

In one experiment in the late 1970s, Dr. Lance Evans of the Brookhaven National Laboratory in New York simulated acid rain's effects on soybeans. He found that acid rain with a pH of 4 caused a 2.6% reduction in seed yield. Other experiments have clearly shown the damaging effects of ozone—acid rain's nitrogen oxide–induced relative—on vegetation. As with trees, ozone enters microscopic pores in vegetation and harms delicate cell membranes. Injuries include yellowing of leaves and death of tissue, decreased growth, reduced yield or quality, and heightened sensitivity to stress.

SOIL

Acid rain's damages in the air are dwarfed by the wounds it inflicts once it reaches the ground. Its effects on soils can be devastating: to trees, which get most of their nutrients from soil; to lakes, ponds, streams, and other waterways, which receive runoff from soils uphill; and to animals, including humans, who drink from those bodies of water, often from pipes from which acids can leach toxic metals.

Some soils have the ability to disarm the acids in acid rain. First, soils with high alkalinity, such as those rich in limestone, can neutralize acids. Second, some soils and vegetation can retain the sulfate and nitrate ions found in sulfuric and nitric acids. Third, *cation exchange* takes place in some soils. In this process, *cations* (positively charged ions) of certain metals, such as magnesium and calcium, that are found in many soils and that fertilize trees, take the place of the hydrogen cation in an

Field workers investigate the effects of acid rain in an experiment on Mount Mitchell. Tree seedlings are isolated and exposed to varying concentrations of atmospheric pollutants.

acid. (These metal cations, along with bicarbonate *anions,* or negatively charged ions, are liberated from rock by the weak carbonic acid that forms naturally in rainwater.)

Positive   and negative charges attract each other. In cation exchange, the hydrogen cation (H) in sulfuric acid (H_2SO_4) or nitric acid (HNO_3) is replaced by a cation of, for example, magnesium, which bonds to the anions of sulfate (SO_4^{2-}) and nitrate (NO_3^-) that are components of sulfuric and nitric acids. When the resulting sulfate or nitrate solution washes out of the soil, taking the metals with it, the hydrogen ions responsible for the acidity are left behind in the soil, where they are neutralized by the bicarbonate anions.

In soils that do not have these buffering or exchange abilities, however, acids can have damaging effects. For example, acids can mobilize aluminum, a metal that is normally locked up harmlessly in aluminum silicates. Like a thief escaped from prison, the freed aluminum then steals binding sites on the fine roots of trees away from calcium and other minerals. Starved of these vital nutrients, the tree's growth slows, a change readily visible in thinner tree rings. Aluminum can also impede the flow of water through a tree, increasing its susceptibility to drought.

Acid rain can also leach vital nutrients directly from the soil and can kill soil bacteria that supply nutrients by breaking down decaying organic material. Nitrate released from nitric acids can injure root-hugging fungi that help to both protect trees from disease and extract water and nutrients from the soil.

Ironically, excess nitrates may initially increase tree growth, because they serve as fertilizers. But too much of a good thing is never healthy. Soon high levels of nitrates simply

In an effort to combat increasing acidification, an alkaline calcium compound called lime is poured from a boat into an Adirondack pond.

overwhelm a tree's capacity to use them, and they pass into the soil, taking essential nutrients with them.

Too much nitrogen (in the form of nitrates) deposited in soil by acid rain may also, it seems, contribute to global warming. Dr. Paul Steudler and colleagues at the Marine Biological Laboratory at Woods Hole, Massachusetts, added ammonium nitrate fertilizer to experimental soil plots and recorded the methane gas caught in plastic boxes above the soil. After six months, the researchers found, the amount of methane above the fertilized plots was one-third higher than in the unfertilized soil, suggesting that the microbes that normally absorb methane—a potent greenhouse gas—preferred to feast on the nitrogen instead.

Steudler and his co-workers concluded that decades of exposure to acid rain and nitrogen fertilizers may greatly inhibit soil's ability to operate as a methane "sink," absorbing methane that would otherwise reside in the atmosphere, intensifying the feared greenhouse effect.

WATER

What happens when acidic runoff from agricultural fields and from untilled land reaches bodies of water, bringing with it all the sulfate, nitrate, and metal ions, including aluminum?

Like soil, lakes and streams may possess a buffering capacity. For instance, they may contain bicarbonate and other basic ions generated by natural rock weathering that can neutralize acids. But even bodies of water with a strong buffering capacity—even those continually renewed by rock weathering—can become overwhelmed by a continual influx of acids. Particularly at risk are lakes in regions with high levels of pollution coupled with thin soils, such as those in the Adirondacks and eastern Canada.

In 1986, the National Academy of Sciences (NAS) compared current pH measurements of several hundred lakes in New York, New Hampshire, and Wisconsin with pH measurements made between the 1920s and 1940s. The academy found that while pH in the New Hampshire lakes stayed about the same and those in Wisconsin rose on average, pH dropped considerably during that time in the lakes in New York, particularly in the Adirondacks, where 6 of 11 lakes tested had fallen to a pH of 5.2. (A National Surface Water Survey in the mid-1980s revealed a high percentage of acidified lakes also in the Pocono Mountains of Pennsylvania and on Michigan's Upper Peninsula, areas where buffering capacity is low and rain often strongly acidic.)

The NAS findings underlie the problem of convincing industry of the dire need to curb emissions that cause acid rain. If all lakes showed acidity and millions of trees across wide swaths of the nation displayed damage, the danger would be obvious. But because many lakes and forests appear healthy, the task of environmentalists and scientists concerned that the problem is far more serious than is readily apparent—and therefore requires immediate action—is daunting.

In the 1970s, the Canadian government, worried about the thousands of acidified, or soon-to-be acidified, lakes in the country's eastern provinces, decided to find out what a rapidly lowering pH would do to a lake and its wildlife. In 1976, Dr. David Schindler and his colleagues at the Freshwater Institute in Winnipeg began pouring sulfuric acid into a lake in western Ontario at a rate sufficient to roughly double the lake's acidity every year. Known simply as Lake 223, the test lake lies on the Canadian Shield, a 2-million-square-mile slab of glacier-scoured granite whose shallow soils and clear lakes are highly sensitive to acidification. Here is what happened to Lake 223:

As the lake's acidity decreased from an original pH of 6.8, its natural alkalinity became overwhelmed, levels of toxic metals such as aluminum increased, and fish began to show signs of stress. By 1978, the pH was 5.8, and a species of copepod, a tiny crustacean that is a key link in the marine food chain, disappeared. The next year, at pH 5.6, a type of shrimp favored by lake trout vanished, and populations of fathead minnows and slimy sculpins declined. By 1980, the pH had dropped to 5.4, and another species of copepod vanished. Three-quarters of the adult crayfish, which had suffered increased difficulty regenerating their hard exoskeletons after each molt, died. (Some species, however, such as the pearl dace, increased temporarily by filling ecological spaces left by the extinction of others, such as the fathead minnow.) By the time the pH reached 5, a third of the species studied had been eliminated.

H U M A N S

From the moment an acidic droplet falls on the highest branch of the tallest tree on a mountaintop to the time it trickles down the tree, percolates through soil, and washes into a lake or

Spring thaws of ice and snow can release large amounts of acids suddenly, making lakes and waterways fatally poisonous for young rainbow trout, called fingerlings.

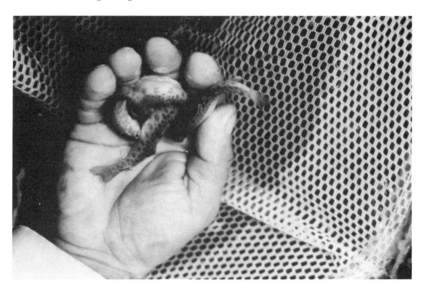

Smog blankets the city of Los Angeles, California. Air pollutants born of fossil-fuel combustion endanger the health of hundreds of millions of people worldwide.

stream, acid rain has little effect on human beings. But once it reaches reservoirs and underground aquifers, it can injure its creators.

Acids make certain heavy metals, such as aluminum, cadmium, and mercury, more soluble. That means water can wash them away more easily. Toxic metals leached from soils and lake sediments eventually reach aquifers, reservoirs, and streams, where they contaminate edible fish and drinking water. In this direct way, acid rain reaches the animals highest in the world's food chain—*Homo sapiens.*

As acidic water makes its way from reservoir to faucet, it can do more damage. In the same way that acids leach heavy metals from soil, they can also leach lead and copper from water-supply pipes and conduits. In certain parts of the United States and Sweden, higher-than-normal levels of toxic metals have been found in the drinking water of areas known to suffer from acid precipitation.

Aluminum can be especially debilitating. In areas where aluminum levels in public water supplies are high, there has been an increase in reported cases of osteomalacia, a rare bone-softening disease, reports Dr. F. H. Barnaby in the journal *Ambio* (1989). Perhaps like the crustaceans in Lake 223 that had trouble regenerating exoskeletons after molting, people with this disease have an impaired bone-forming ability.

Before it even reaches the ground, acid rain–inducing air pollution can have serious effects on humans. Before it causes acid rain, sulfur dioxide can chemically transform into tiny sulfate particles. In the air, these particles combine with water to form aerosols, or particle-containing mists, that people can easily breathe deep into their lungs, bringing toxic metals and gases with them. Once inside the body, reports the Worldwatch Institute, these pollutants can raise the incidence of acute respiratory diseases, including colds, asthma, bronchitis, and emphysema. Sulfur dioxide can also aggravate symptoms of heart disease.

Some researchers, as reported in a U.S. Office of Technology Assessment document, contend that a mixture of sulfates, toxic metals, and poisonous gases may be responsible for as many as 50,000 deaths in the United States each year, or 2% of the nation's annual mortality. Although deaths are the worst manifestation, nonfatal injuries from air pollution are far more common. According to the EPA, 150 million people in the United States breathe air considered unhealthy by that government agency. In fact, Thomas Crocker of the University of Wyoming estimates that air pollution costs the United States $40 billion a year in health care and lost productivity.

Around the world, the picture is even more dismal. The World Health Organization and the United Nations Environment Program estimate that nearly 625 million people around the world are exposed to unhealthy levels of sulfur dioxide and more than 1 billion to dangerous levels of suspended particulates. (Whereas sulfur and nitrogen oxides are gaseous pollutants, particulates are solid specks of pollution that are so minuscule that they are practically "lighter than air.")

Finally, ozone, which shields the earth from harmful ultraviolet radiation from the sun when it exists high in the atmosphere, can cause short-term breathing difficulty and long-term lung damage down on the ground, where it is known as ground-level ozone, the primary component of photochemical smog (from "smoke" and "fog"). (Ground-level ozone is created by the action of sunlight upon air pollution.) Most major cities in the United States now have "smog alerts," warning citizens to avoid the outdoors on days when levels of ozone or other pollutants are excessive.

MONUMENTAL DECAY

Damage from acid rain is not restricted to living things. Acid rain eats away at buildings, monuments, bridges, statues, and other artifacts of the human race.

Acids work their destruction in various ways. Sulfuric and nitric acids already formed in the atmosphere can adhere to surfaces by dry deposition, by rainfall, or by fogs and dew ("occult deposition"). Or acids can be formed on the surface itself. In a process known as *sulfation*, researchers in Greece and England have found that sulfur dioxide or sulfur trioxide (SO_3) can react with wet limestone (calcium carbonate) to create sulfuric acid. The acid then transforms the limestone into more soluble gypsum (calcium sulfate), which rain can erode more easily. Even pure rain, because of its weak carbonic acid content, can convert limestone or chalk into water-soluble calcium bicarbonate.

Acids can also create salts that can trigger other mechanisms of stone decay. As salts crystallize, they can force apart mineral grains, causing stone to disintegrate. Or, as temperatures rise and fall and salts absorb and shed moisture, salts can expand and contract and thereby weather surfaces.

Finally, the same industrial and domestic sources that produce sulfur and nitrogen oxides seem to be responsible for *black crusts*, the dark deposits of particulates such as soot that

Many scientists and art historians believe that acid rain is destroying such ancient treasures as the Temple of the Frescoes, among the Maya ruins at Tulum, Mexico.

often blanket buildings in industrialized regions around the world, especially rain- and wind-protected areas beneath ledges or in the midst of architectural decoration. Soot particles are catalysts for crystallization or conversion to gypsum, processes that are both blamed for severe decay.

Much of the research into stone breakdown has been done by researchers at the Laboratorio Scientifico della Misericordia in Venice, Italy, where black crusts have disfigured the creamy-white Istrian limestone and lovely Italian marble of such architectural treasures as the Ducal Palace. Black crusts have also scabbed ancient Maya palaces on the Yucatán Peninsula, where acid rain born of pollution billowing from uncapped Mexican oil wells and oil-field smokestacks nearby is corroding 750-to-1,500-year-old temples and causing paint from pre-Columbian frescoes to peel off by the handful. Nitrogen oxides also play a part. Dr. Merle Greene Robertson, director of San Francisco's Pre-Columbian Art Research Institute, found that tour buses parked for hours with their engines running were behind the rapid deterioration of painted walls at the Temple of the Frescoes at Tulum. After a three-year study, Robertson concluded ominously that "the sculpture and architecture of the Maya civilization are being destroyed by acidic precipitation."

Acids seem to deface all kinds of building materials. In the United States, proud symbols of American heritage, including the stone monuments at Gettysburg, the granite-and-marble Washington Monument, the copper Statue of Liberty, and the brick Independence Hall in Philadelphia, have all suffered from acid rain. In Greece, classical marble architecture is taking a horrible beating. T. N. Skoulikidis, a Greek acid-corrosion expert, has estimated that the ancient monuments of Athens, including the world-famous Parthenon, have deteriorated more in the past 20 to 25 years from pollution than in the previous 2,400 years. In the words of *New York Times* correspondent Paul Hoffmann, "Classic marble busts are being transmogrified into noseless and earless plaster grotesques."

This deterioration does not happen all at once. As Dr. Bernard Smith and colleagues wrote in an article in *New Scientist* (June 2, 1988), "Decay is not a steady, continuous loss of material: for many years, there may be little visible cracking or erosion. The rock then reaches a critical threshold and fails."

Such "hidden" damages may be the most insidious aspect of acid rain. And it is true not only of structures. Lakes suffering from increasing acid inputs may appear fine until suddenly their buffering capacity becomes overwhelmed and they turn acidic. Fishermen often report large catches in acidified lakes where fish have long since lost the ability to reproduce. Forests and even individual trees can appear healthy until a simple examination of tree rings reveals severely impaired growth.

Even though some of acid rain's effects are becoming painfully obvious, many remain too subtle or ambiguous to elicit immediate action. Until clear connections can be made between acid rain and the living and nonliving things it appears to threaten, societies around the world, it seems, will continue to neglect this problem. Sadly, yet significantly, the damage is becoming hard to ignore.

The effects of various air pollutants are visible on this young fir growing beside a much-traveled highway on Whiteface Mountain, New York.

F A L L O U T   O V E R   N O R T H   A M E R I C A

The northeastern portion of the United States and Canada has been called the "atmospheric garbage dump" of North America. The bulk of the air pollution created in the most heavily industrialized region of the continent winds up here. Not surprisingly, this slab of the vast Canadian Shield is suffering some of the most serious environmental effects from acid fallout of any area on the planet.

In the northeastern United States, both deciduous and evergreen trees—including sugar maple, yellow birch, white birch, American beech, white ash, white spruce, and balsam fir—appear to be declining. For several decades, scientists have noticed shorter needles, lower heights, and smaller diameters in white pine trees. Red spruce seem to be the worst hit: Above 2,500 feet, half of the red spruce that seemed healthy in the early 1960s are now dead, according to James MacKenzie of the World Resources Institute.

As previously discussed, high-altitude regions suffer worse than those at lower altitudes. On Whiteface Mountain in the Adirondacks, the lowest recorded pH was 2.8. On Whitetop

Mountain in Virginia, it was 2.6, and between April and November 1986, researchers found, the amount of sulfate landing on the mountain was 10 times that falling on lower elevations.

Acid rain is also threatening soils, and not just on the acid-sensitive Canadian Shield. In a 1986 study of soil chemistry in forests, researchers at the Oak Ridge National Laboratory in Tennessee found that 41% of soils in the eastern United States are susceptible to considerable nutrient leaching and thus to forest decline.

ACID LAKES

Runoff from these soils, as well as direct hits by acid rain, are acidifying lakes across the country. The Environmental Defense Fund estimates that about 1,000 lakes in the United States are very acidified and that 3,000 are marginally acidified. Another report, produced by the federal Office of Technology Assessment, figured that approximately 9,400 eastern lakes (plus or minus 20%) had poor buffering capacities—either because they did not have much neutralizing capacity to begin with or because that capacity had been strained by acidification. In addition, 51,000 miles of streams in the eastern part of the country were categorized by the report as "already altered or seriously at risk."

For lakes, being "seriously at risk" means more than just having acidic water. Fish that ply such waters are being forced to drink acid in such quantities that they are dying by the thousands, in some cases disappearing from lakes and streams altogether. Such local extinctions are occurring in states up and down the eastern seaboard.

Long before fish are lost, however, insects and other lower life-forms that are critical players in the marine ecosystem vanish. In fact, the Freshwater Institute's David Schindler and colleagues, who conducted the Lake 223 study, correlated data from that and other studies with the chemical lowdown on 6,351 U.S. lakes identified by the EPA's Eastern Lakes Survey as being sensitive to acids. The researchers concluded that lakes in the Adirondack, Catskill, and Pocono mountains may already have lost 69% of their leeches, 50% of mollusks (e.g., snails and clams), 45% of insects, 18% of crustaceans (e.g., crabs, shrimp, and water fleas), and up to 30% of algae.

The loss of these fauna and flora spells doom for those higher up on the food chain. In the Adirondacks, one-fourth of the lakes and ponds are so acidic that they can no longer support fish life, reports the New York State Department of Environmental Conservation. Another fifth may soon be equally toxic if acid inputs are not controlled. Not surprisingly, most of the acidic lakes are found above 2,000 feet in the southwestern Adirondacks, an area directly downwind of pollution sources.

If the prevailing winds blow the Ohio Valley's pollution a bit more to the south, Pennsylvania gets the brunt of it. In 1987, the Pennsylvania Fish Commission estimated that fully half the state's streams will be unable to support fish life by the turn of the century if acid fallout continues unabated.

WETLAND WILDLIFE

Coastal waters also suffer. A 1988 study by the Environmental Defense Fund showed that one-fourth of the nitrogen entering Chesapeake Bay, the largest estuary in the

Canoeists ply the waters of Chesapeake Bay. Fish populations in the bay are now threatened by algal blooms caused by excessive nitrogen.

United States, comes from airborne nitrate pollutants. Too much nitrogen causes algal blooms, a process known as *eutrophication*. These algae cut off sunlight and reduce oxygen supplies needed by other plants and animals. If emissions continue at their present rate, the study found, airborne nitrate will contribute 42% of the bay's incoming nitrogen by the year 2030.

Some species of migratory birds may suffer indirectly from acidified coastal waters. A report by the Izaak Walton League of America held that the dramatic decline of North American black ducks since the 1950s may be caused by a reduction of invertebrate food supplies in acidified wetlands. Adult ducks usually thrive on plants, but young ducks and egg-laying females need animal protein. Unfortunately, eggs hatch in springtime, just when acidity is highest in North American waterways—and food supplies lowest. As a result, reports a U.S. Fish and Wildlife Service study, ducklings are three times more likely to perish before attaining adulthood if reared on acidified waters.

TAP WATER

Drinking-water supplies are also endangered. The enormous Quabbin Reservoir in Massachusetts, which supplies drinking water for millions of people in and around Boston, has lost three-fourths of its acid-buffering capacity and may lose the rest within 20 years, according to the Massachusetts Executive Office of Environmental Affairs. (Dick Keller of the state's Division of Fish and Wildlife warned in the early 1980s that the Quabbin, which supports a $1-million-a-year sports fishery, could also lose its fish populations within the next decade.) Overall, more than half of Massachusetts's 34 drinking-water reservoirs have lost the balance of their acid-neutralizing capacity since 1940.

Incidents of acids leaching dangerous metals from plumbing have also been reported. In Bennington, Vermont,

Black ducks and other wildlife face severe food shortages in acidified waters, particularly in springtime.

acid-laden water taken from Bolles Brook leached lead from water pipes supplying drinking water to some of the town's residents. In 1979, the town spent $37,000 for sodium bicarbonate and sodium hydroxide to reduce acidity and so lower the water's lead levels. In Massachusetts, the Metropolitan District Commission similarly spent $469,000 to raise the pH of drinking water in the Boston area.

SOUTHERN EXTREMES

Some areas of the southeastern United States are as hard hit as the Northeast. North Carolina, Tennessee, and Virginia, for example, possess 66,000 acres of spruce-fir forests. On a quarter of this land, reports the World Resources Institute's James MacKenzie, more than 70% of the standing trees are now dead. Studies have shown that throughout mountainous regions of the Southeast, the radial growth rates of most yellow pines less than 16 inches in diameter have declined by 30% to 50% in the past 3 decades, and furthermore, the death rate of these trees rose from 9% a year in 1975 to 15% just 10 years later.

In fact, a 1981 study by the National Wildlife Federation (NWF) showed most clearly how all 27 states east of the Mississippi River are vulnerable to attack by acidic rainfall. In every state, the average pH of rainfall was between 4.1 and 4.7, and every state except Florida, Georgia, and Mississippi witnessed some rainfall with a pH below 4. On a five-level scale from "not vulnerable" to "extremely vulnerable," the study found that fisheries, soils, and masonry (stone- or brickwork) in most states were either "extremely" or "moderately" vulnerable—the two highest levels. In an overall ranking, the study found 15 states "extremely," 10 states "moderately," and only 1 state "slightly" vulnerable. (For the state of Louisiana, there were insufficient data.)

THE FARM BELT

The NWF study reported that crops, on the other hand, were deemed in most eastern states either "vulnerable" or "not vulnerable"—the two lowest categories. However, a bit farther to the west, in the country's farm belt, certain major crops are growing slower than they should be or have leaves that are deformed or discolored. As previously mentioned, researchers believe acid rain may work in conjunction with ozone to damage crops.

According to a 1987 study by the U.S. government's National Acid Precipitation Assessment Program, current levels of ozone were reducing crop yields by 1% or less for sorghum and corn, by about 7% for cotton and soybeans, and by more than 30% for alfalfa. What role acid rain played is not known, but total crop losses added up to 5% to 10% of production. Walter Heck of the Department of Agriculture's Air Quality Research Program estimated that a halving of ozone levels would result in an increase in the output of 4 major crops—soybeans, corn, wheat, and peanuts—worth up to $5 billion.

GREAT LAKES

When winds blow west rather than east, the Great Lakes region takes an acid lashing. In Wisconsin, 2,600 lakes, each larger than 20 acres, have been deemed very susceptible because their pH is 6 or lower and they have little overall alkalinity. In

In an experiment at the Medicine Bow National Forest in Wyoming, seedlings are studied for signs of stress from airborne pollutants.

Michigan, 16,000 lakes, each more than 10 acres in size, are considered susceptible. In Minnesota, often called the Land of 10,000 Lakes, U.S. and Canadian scientists wrote in a 1981 report that "atmosphere loadings [i.e., concentrations of pollutants] near the Boundary Waters Canoe Area Wilderness [on the state's border with Ontario] are at levels associated with the onset of lake acidification in Scandinavia." Based on this comparison, the report concluded, acid rain was probably already affecting the most vulnerable lakes in the Minnesota waters studied.

THE ROCKY MOUNTAINS AND WESTWARD

Even the soaring, snowcapped peaks of the Rocky Mountains are not immune to acid rain. While working at the University of Colorado's Mountain Research Station, located at an altitude of 9,000 feet in Colorado's Front Range, Drs. William Lewis, Jr., and Michael Grant discovered that the pH of rain fell rapidly between 1974 and 1978, from 5.4 to 5.0 to 4.8 to 4.7. As lakes in the Rockies, as in the Adirondacks, tend to lie over granite and therefore possess little buffering strength, Lewis and Grant believe these lakes will be affected sooner and more adversely than the region's forests and other land ecosystems.

Even those western states seemingly far removed from industrial regions have acidic rainfall. Robert Boyle and R. Alexander Boyle wrote in their book *Acid Rain* that in 1980 rainfall pH averaged 5.2 in Yellowstone National Park in Wyoming, 4.9 in Glacier National Park in Montana, and 4.8 at Craters of the Moon National Monument in Idaho. And these measurements are of wet deposition—such as rain and snow—only, not dry deposition, which may worsen the problem, they wrote.

Because prevailing winds generally blow from west to east across the United States, most pollution that reaches the farthest-west states probably originates in factories and automobiles along the West Coast. A coal-fired power plant and a smelter in the Puget Sound area are a big source of western Washington State's pollution, say Drs. Eugene Welch and William Chamberlain of the University of Washington. In a 1981 report to the National Park Service, they noted that the pH of rain falling on Seattle ranged from 5.2 to 4.2 about 70% of the time. The researchers also found that more than one-third of the lakes they measured in the Cascades and the Olympic Mountains registered a pH of less than 6; at least 7 lakes in the Cascades fell below 5.5.

Farther south, in California, lakes are faring similarly. Kathy Tonnessen and John Harte of the Berkeley Lawrence

Lake McDonald, in Glacier National Park, Montana. Even this remote part of the West suffers from highly acidic rainfall.

Laboratory have found lakes in the Sierra Nevada with pHs of 5.8 and high levels of aluminum. Pasadena holds the dubious distinction of having weathered California's most acidic rainfall: Dr. James Morgan of the California Institute of Technology measured a light drizzle in November 1978 at pH 2.9.

Near San Bernadino, 75 miles east of the heavily polluted Los Angeles Basin in which Pasadena rests, 6% to 10% of ponderosa and Jeffrey pines died in a 6-year period. In the early 1950s, when damage to these trees first appeared, scientists conducted a revealing experiment. They enclosed branches of some of these damaged trees in three test chambers—one containing the area's typical ozone-rich air, another filtered air, and a third a combination of ozone-rich and filtered air. The branches in the filtered air improved, while the other two continued to decline.

CALAMITY IN CANADA

When the last of the Wisconsin glaciers retreated at the close of the last ice age, they scoured the landscape of northeastern North America clear of all vegetation, soil, and loose rock. Scars from rocks embedded in the base of retreating glaciers can still be seen on the subalpine summits of mountains from Maine to the Adirondacks and up into eastern Canada.

In the roughly 10,000 years since then, only a thin layer of soil has regenerated to cover this Precambrian granite, known as the Canadian Shield. As a result, the soil and lakes lying on top of the Shield have little capacity to buffer excess acids. In fact, Canada's lakes are hurting about as badly as those in Scandinavia, which suffers the similar fate of being at the receiving end of thousands of tons of airborne pollutants originating beyond its borders.

If Minnesota is the Land of 10,000 Lakes, Canada might be called the Land of 1,000,000 Lakes. Sadly, hundreds of thousands of these are already acidic or threatened with becoming so. According to a 1989 Environmental and Energy Study Institute Special Report, more than 14,000 Canadian lakes are strongly acidified, and 150,000—1 in 7—in the eastern part of Canada suffer biological damage. The Worldwatch Institute reports that 350,000 lakes in Canada's 6 eastern provinces are highly acid sensitive, as are significant portions of lakes in the Yukon, Northwest Territories, Labrador, and the country's western provinces.

In the province of Ontario, for example, the Ontario Ministry of the Environment estimates that as a result of acid fallout, fish populations in that province have declined in 1,200 lakes and may begin to decline in up to 15,000 more. Worse, the ministry predicts that if current emission rates continue, 48,500 of its lakes could lose their fish populations in the next 20 years.

In particular, acidity threatens eastern Canada's lucrative Atlantic salmon-fishing industry. Nova Scotia is a case in point. Dr. Walton Watt of Canada's Department of Fisheries and Oceans in Halifax reports that 10 Nova Scotian salmon rivers are so acidic that they are unable to support fish life. Eight of these register a pH of below 4.7, and 20 more Nova Scotian salmon rivers have pHs ranging from 4.7 to 5.4. Angling records going

Beginning in 1986, a site on an acidic Canadian river was limed to raise the water's pH level; by 1990, the young salmon population was restored to normal.

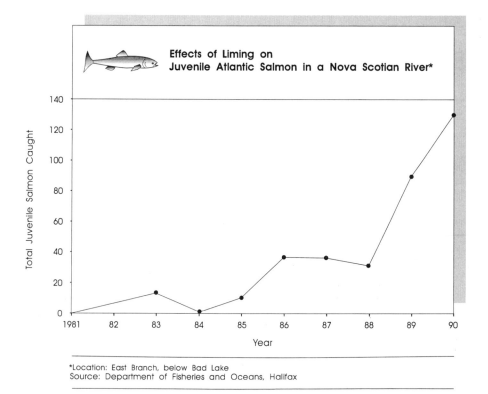

*Location: East Branch, below Bad Lake
Source: Department of Fisheries and Oceans, Halifax

back more than a century for several of these rivers, reports Watt, show regular catches until the 1950s, followed by a steady decline. By 1970, anglers bagged virtually no fish, and salmon runs there are now considered extinct, says Watt.

Canada's lucrative logging industry is also at risk. As Sandra Postel of the Worldwatch Institute has observed, "With 1 out of every 10 Canadian jobs dependent on the forest industry, and annual forest products valued at more than $20 billion, Canadian officials are understandably concerned about acid deposition's potential to damage their timber supply."

Many leaders in industries responsible for acidic pollution feel the verdict is still out on whether pollution causes tree declines. Yet regarding the danger to Canada's forests, Dr. F. H. Bormann of Yale University warns, "The danger is that by the time a 15 to 20 percent loss in productivity has been documented, degradation will be irreversible."

"If a hostile power were doing to us what we are doing to Canada, the Congress would now be meeting to consider a declaration of war," write the Boyles in *Acid Rain*. Although that may be overstated, the seriousness of the problem—and the dispute between the two giant neighbors—is not. The transboundary problem may be graver still in Europe, where 10 times as many countries are involved and the impact on all fronts has been far more devastating than in North America.

A desolate outcropping of trees in a Czechoslovakian forest. The acid scourge has been severe in Eastern European countries.

chapter 5

GLOBAL DISASTER

The Chernobyl nuclear disaster in April 1986 sent clouds of radiation into nearby Scandinavia. But that was an isolated event. Every day, all year long, air pollutants from neighboring countries blow into Scandinavia. According to the Worldwatch Institute, Norway and Sweden receive 96% and 89%, respectively, of their sulfur pollution from other countries.

Effects from that never-ending barrage have been severe in Scandinavia, particularly on aquatic ecosystems. In Sweden, where researcher Svante Odén first successfully brought the acid rain issue to the world's attention in the late 1960s, 14,000 lakes can no longer support sensitive aquatic life, and 2,200 show virtually no signs of life, according to the United Nations Economic Commission for Europe (ECE).

In Finland, a recent survey of 1,000 lakes showed that a significant number throughout the country have a low buffering capacity; 8% of the lakes studied have no neutralizing capacity at all. Although severe effects have not yet been reported in Denmark, that nation has been added to the list of European countries with acid-sensitive waters.

In Norway, the "Thousand Lakes Survey" revealed that an already shocking situation in the mid-1970s had grown steadily worse by the mid-1980s. Data collected between 1974 and 1979 showed 8,000 square miles of lakes "almost totally damaged"— that is, having most wildlife gone, including all fish. That figure rose to approximately 11,000 square miles by 1986, when the survey was done. All told, the survey reported that more than 22,000 square miles of lakes—almost a third of Norway—are affected by acid rain.

Not surprisingly, the most seriously affected region is southernmost Norway, which is equidistant from sulfur dioxide–gushing factories in the United Kingdom and Ireland to the southwest and eastern Europe to the southeast. Dr. Arne Henricksen, a chemist at the Norwegian Institute for Water Research in Oslo, and his colleagues determined during the study that the number of barren lakes in southern Norway had doubled between the early 1970s and 1986. Approximately half of the lakes surveyed were threatened by acidification, the team found, yet over half of these (28%) would be able to recover with a 30% drop in sulfur loadings; a 50% drop would enable fish to repopulate 40% of these lakes. (Most European nations have agreed to slash sulfur dioxide emissions by 30% to 50% by 1995; see Chapter 7.)

The Scandinavian governments feel that much of their pollution originates in the United Kingdom. The U.K. releases more sulfur dioxide than does any other European country (save the Soviet Union), a total of 3,680,000 tons in 1987. Prevailing west-to-east winds carry much of that due eastward onto the

European continent, yet the U.K. also suffers from its own emissions. In a 1985 survey, the environmental organization Friends of the Earth reported that about 70% of all British beech trees and 80% of all yew trees showed signs of injury associated with acid rain. Britain's soils are not seriously at risk because they have a high neutralizing capacity. But there are acidified lakes in southwestern Scotland, in western Wales, and in England's celebrated Lake District. In some acidified Welsh streams, researchers have discovered, populations of birds called dippers have declined.

Dutch environmentalists have chalked crosses on trees along highways in the Netherlands in an attempt to heighten motorists' awareness of the acid rain problem.

The list of European countries whose waters have been affected by acidic debris now also includes Ireland, Belgium, the Netherlands, Italy, Switzerland, and Germany. Yet central Europe faces a much greater threat to its forests. Indeed, the Germans have coined a word for the lethal effect acid rain has on many of its woodlands: *Waldsterben,* or "forest death."

Germany's forests have apparently suffered more than those of any other country, in Europe or elsewhere. In fact, Germany first sounded the alarm about its dying forests in the early 1980s. In what was then West Germany, a 1982 survey by the German Federal Minister of Food, Agriculture, and Forestry estimated that 8% of the country's 7.4 million hectares of forests—an area covering about a third of West Germany's land area—were damaged. That figure rose to 34% in 1983, to 50% in 1984, and to 54% in 1986, partially because concern led to a more extensive survey. The percentage has since declined to 52% in 1988—still more than half of the forests of what is now the western portion of Germany. In some areas, all mature trees are dead. (There are no figures as yet for the area formerly known as East Germany, but considering Eastern Europe's pollution track record, the wounds may be even deeper.)

As in the eastern United States, conifers appear especially hard hit in Germany. In 1983, German scientists found that 75% of firs and well over a third of both pine and spruce—the latter being the forest industry's most important species—showed blemishes. Hardwoods such as beech and oak have also suffered.

One of the best-studied areas in Germany is Fichtelgebirge, a high-altitude forest in Bavaria. Scientists first began to notice damage there in the late 1970s, when conifer needles turned yellow and fell off—in springtime, no less. Since then, the rate of decline has been shockingly steep. In 1978, a stand of 130-year-old trees growing on Fichtelgebirge's highest mountain appeared robust, according to Dr. Ernst-Detlef Schulze, who heads the team of ecologists studying the Bavarian woodland. By 1983, heavy needle loss was evident, and by 1988, all the trees were dead.

The bad news from Germany led other countries throughout Europe to assess the damage to their own forests. A 1988 ECE report revealed that in at least 11 western European nations, an estimated one-third or more of forests were damaged. In descending order of magnitude of injury, these included Greece, the United Kingdom, West Germany, Liechtenstein, Norway, Denmark, the Netherlands, Switzerland, Luxembourg, Finland, and Sweden. Parts of Belgium and Italy surveyed also showed a similar amount of affliction, and France, Austria, Spain, and Portugal announced a smaller yet still significant percentage of damage.

EASTERN EUROPE'S PLIGHT

Eastern European forests are also threatened, according to the ECE study. Czechoslovakia topped the ECE list, with 71% of its woodlands scarred by acid rain. In the fabled forests of Bohemia, in northwest Czechoslovakia, ecologist Josef Krecek, who with Western assistance is undertaking one of Eastern Europe's first assessments of the acid scourge, estimates that one-fifth of the towering Norway spruces and European beeches that blanket the region are injured.

Czechoslovakia has also been forthcoming about the health effects of Eastern Europe's severe air pollution. At a European Community environment meeting held in Ireland in 1990, the Czech environment minister, Josef Vavrousek, claimed that his country's pollution was the world's worst, with sulfur dioxide levels in Prague and Bohemia sometimes 20 times higher than the national norm. Life expectancy, he said, has fallen to between five and seven years lower than that of Western Europe's citizens; in heavily industrialized Bohemia, that figure is 11 years lower, he says.

The ECE environmental report listed other Eastern European nations with marred forests, including Poland (49%),

Soviet scientists examine a felled tree in a boreal, or northern, forest for evidence of climate change. Glasnost has allowed the rest of the world more access to information on environmental problems in the USSR.

East Germany (44%), Bulgaria (43%), Yugoslavia (32%), and Hungary (22%). For all of Europe, based on information gathered by the ECE, the Worldwatch Institute estimated in 1990 that nearly 50 million hectares—or roughly 35% of Europe's total forested area—have been damaged. Increasingly, the evidence points toward acid rain as the key factor in this decline.

THE SOVIET UNION

The ECE report also mentioned Estonia and Lithuania, which, though politically part of the Soviet Union, are considered geographically to be part of Europe. More than half the 1,795 hectares of Estonian woodlands and one-fifth of Lithuania's 1,810 hectares show deterioration.

Over the years, the Soviet Union, as is typical of communist-led countries, has been extremely reticent about releasing information concerning possible acid rain abuse in its lands. Yet through *glasnost*, or "openness," a recent demo-cratizing of its political process, the Soviet Union has begun to own up to such abuses.

"One might say that for a whole era our party and professional propaganda and science have been intolerably passive as far as ecology is concerned," said Fyodor Morgun, chairman of the Soviet Union's State Committee for En-vironmental Protection, in 1988. "For many decades, the environment has been undergoing catastrophic pollution." He added that 50 million Soviet citizens in 102 cities are exposed to pollutants *10 times* higher than the national standards.

Valentin Sokolovsky, first deputy of the committee, emphasized that his nation suffered from acid rain blowing into the Soviet Union from other countries. He did not specify to what degree it suffered or to what foreign lands the Soviet Union owes its import of pollutants. But the new openness, spurred by glasnost, has led the Soviets to acknowledge some role in the pollution problem. Indeed, another committee deputy, Guennady Biryukov, admitted that significant emissions from Soviet nickel-smelting plants blew into Norway. (As mentioned in Chapter 3, U.S. scientists also believe Soviet and European emissions waft all the way to Alaska via the North Pole.)

CHINA'S DYING FORESTS

The People's Republic of China has also been notoriously closemouthed about anything bad taking place within its borders. Yet it too has recently begun to open up about heavy damage to forests in its southwestern provinces.

In May 1989, China's *Science and Technology Daily* reported that acid rain was causing about 1 billion yuan ($260 million at 1989 exchange rates) in crop damages in Hunan Province. In Chongqing, the largest city in southwestern China, more than half of the masson pines in an 1,800-hectare forest on Nanshan Hill have died, according to the Worldwatch Institute. In the province's Maocaoba pine forest, more than 90% of the trees are now dead. Covering 5,400 hectares, the trees, it appears, have fallen victim to high levels of sulfur dioxide emitted from hundreds of country, village, and even individual processing plants surrounding a high-sulfur coal mine deep within the forest.

Chen Zhiyuan of China's National Environmental Protection Agency reports that rainfall in Sichuan and neighboring Guizhou Province ranges in acidity from pH 4 to 4.5. The acidity would be much greater, save that the atmosphere over China is high in neutralizing agents, such as ammonium (from human waste used as agricultural fertilizer) and calcium (from small furnaces and limestone in building materials). These may lower the pH but not the amount of sulfate ions, which on their own can cause soil acidification. Guiyang, Guizhou's capital, has 6 times the sulfate ion concentration of New York City and more than 100 times that of a remote area in Australia, reported a joint team of U.S. and Chinese researchers.

Whereas coal in Guizhou is 3% to 5% sulfur, that around Beijing is just 1% sulfur, which may be one reason why southwestern China has been harder hit, ecologically speaking. Yet China as a whole would seem to have a lot to worry about from sulfate deposition. In a study conducted by the United Nations Environment Program and the World Health Organization, 3 of the cities on a list of the 10 cities worldwide with the highest sulfur dioxide concentrations were Chinese: Shenyang, Xi'an, and Beijing. Furthermore, between 1949 and 1982, China increased its use of coal more than twentyfold. In 1982, the nation mined 666 million tons of coal, second only to the United States. By the year 2000, if all goes according to plan, China will double its use of coal.

ACROSS THE THIRD WORLD

India, the world's second most populous nation, also has a dismal pollution picture. According to a report in the *Journal of the Air Pollution Control Association*, sulfur dioxide emissions from coal and oil nearly tripled in that country between the early 1960s and the late 1970s.

One of the most polluted spots in the world for many years was the town of Cubatao, Brazil, where dozens of factories spewed tons of pollutants into the air. Recent clean-up efforts have improved conditions in the region, once nicknamed the Valley of Death.

Across Asia, the United Nations estimates, the population will have expanded from about 2.7 billion in 1985 to 4.2 billion in 2020—by far the largest population increase the world will witness. Latin America and Africa, scientists predict, will more than double their populations. By contrast, the populations of North America and Europe will increase only slightly.

Based on these estimates of population growth, Dr. James Galloway of the University of Virginia believes that although acid rain–causing pollution will not worsen appreciably in North America and Europe in the coming decades, it will in Asia, Africa, and Latin America. "Given the reality of population growth in these areas and the potential for industrial expansion," he says, "future emissions of SO_2 and NOx could greatly exceed current emissions to the global atmosphere."

The ecological threat that such an increase holds for Third World countries is already surfacing. Reports of local damage to trees and crops have come out of Chile, Brazil, and Mexico. A study by the Scientific Committee on Problems of the Environment (SCOPE), under the auspices of the International Council of Scientific Unions, also found that surface waters and soils are highly sensitive to acidification in Venezuela, where a substantial increase in emissions of sulfur and nitrogen has occurred in the past 15 years. Other acid-sensitive problem areas of tomorrow, the report maintained, include parts of southern China and Southeast Asia, southwestern India, southeastern Brazil, and equatorial Africa.

The SCOPE study also monitored high levels of acidity and ozone that are associated with the burning of biomass in the tropics. (Biomass refers to plant or animal matter used as fuel, or to the total weight of living matter in a given area.) In Latin America, for example, farmers cut down and burn tropical rain forests to make room for cattle pasture. Similar high levels in Africa are attributed to the burning each year of what the World Resources Institute estimates is three-quarters of Africa's 591 million hectares of savanna by farmers and herders seeking to clear shrubs and dead vegetation to stimulate growth of crops and grass for ranching.

In fact, researchers at Germany's Max Planck Institute for Chemistry in Mainz found that the burning of African savanna contributes three to four times the carbon dioxide and other trace

gases that tropical deforestation does. Acid rain produced by
savanna burning descends over tropical rain forests throughout
the continent. High levels of pollutants have been found in the
forests of Gabon and Zaire, as well as the Ivory Coast and the
Congo, where French researchers have measured acid rain at pH
4.4 to 4.6.

Most experts feel that a shift in concern over acid rain
is now taking place. Although the United States and Europe
are currently the world's worst polluters—and are now bear-
ing the brunt of acid rain's toll on ecosystems, wildlife, and

*The burning of tropical rainforests and savanna for farming and ranching
contributes to acid rain as well as to a suspected global warming.*

buildings—these nations have made and continue to make significant strides in reducing harmful emissions, mostly in new technology to remove pollutants at the source. In the 21st century, however, it will probably be underdeveloped nations, with their exploding populations and perennial lack of money and technology, that will face the gravest threat from acid rain.

One new coal-conversion technology is a steam-dried coal slurry feed system that turns solid coal into a more energy-efficient liquid fuel.

chapter 6

CLEANING RAIN

Although the price of cutting dangerous, acid rain–causing emissions from utilities, refineries, and even the family car may be staggering, makers and users of all these technologies are increasingly being forced—by governmental decree fueled by public demand—to clean up their act. Some techniques for lowering emissions are proven, others are experimental. Some require new technology, others require alternative fuels. Most are costly in terms of time and the expense of development. What follows is a look at the latest technologies and techniques under discussion and development for slashing releases of sulfur dioxide, nitrogen oxides, and other chemicals that cause acid rain.

PARTICULATES

After incidents such as London's "black fog," which killed thousands in the space of a few days, governments around the world realized the extreme danger posed by particulates. As mentioned previously, while sulfur dioxide and nitrogen oxides are gases, particulates are a varying brew of tiny suspended particles of pollution that can carry toxic metals deep into the lungs.

Because of their demonstrated danger, the most widespread antipollution technology is that used to curb particulate emissions. The two most common technologies are *electrostatic precipitators* and *baghouse filters*. Virtually all member countries within the Organization for Economic Cooperation and Development are required to use these filters, which can reduce the amount of particulates spewing from smokestacks by as much as 99.5%.

Yet there are two drawbacks to this technology. First, it is extremely expensive, so many Third World countries simply do not have the financial means to incorporate it. The United Nations Environment Program and the World Health Organization estimate that, years after particulate-reduction technology became available, a billion people—one out of every five human beings on earth—are still regularly exposed to excessive levels of particulates. Much of these particulates originate in the engines of cars lacking even elementary pollution controls.

The second drawback is that particulate-reduction techniques do nothing to reduce gaseous emissions of sulfur and nitrogen oxides. So industry has come up with a host of new technologies that stop harmful releases at power plants before, during, or after the burning of fossil fuels. Many of these are so-called clean-coal technologies, which, though still largely in the experimental stage, offer significant reductions of both sulfur dioxide and nitrogen oxides while improving energy efficiency—all by cleaning the coal of its sulfur and nitrogen pollutants before and during combustion. (*Note*: Unless otherwise stated, all percentage estimates in this chapter are from the U.S. Department of Energy.)

CLEANSING COAL

Coal, which usually has a sulfur content of between 1% and 6%, can be cleaned of its polluting sulfur before burning by physical, chemical, and biological means. *Physical* cleaning involves pulverizing coal into a sandlike consistency, then washing it of any impurities. Physical cleaning can purge 20% to 50% of the coal's pyritic content—that is, sulfur that is not chemically bound to the coal.

Chemical means can be used to detach organic sulfur that cannot be forced out by physical means. In this case, a chemical

A heating plant at the Argonne National Laboratory in Argonne, Illinois, is outfitted with a dry scrubber and baghouse filter to remove pollutants from the plant's flue gas.

reaction is initiated that alters the molecular form of the organic sulfur, making it more easily separated and eliminated. Chemical cleaning results in a 10% to 30% sulfur reduction. Similarly, *bacterial* cleaning changes the molecular structure of coal and makes it easier to withdraw the sulfur, but by biological means. This process also removes between 10% and 30% of sulfur.

Perhaps the most promising of the clean-coal techniques, *fluidized bed combustion* (FBC), is performed while coal is burned to produce electricity. In this technique, crushed coal and limestone are injected into a large container called a combustor, where incineration will take place. When hot air blown into the combustor reaches a certain speed, the coal and limestone particles take on a "fluidized," or flowing, motion, which mixes them thoroughly. As the coal ignites, the limestone absorbs the sulfur oxides produced. The sulfur-laden limestone settles to the bottom of the combustor as solid ash waste or is collected as lighter-than-air fly ash at the top of the container, where it is carried by superheated gases.

FBC promises a much higher rate of return than do precombustion methods. The amount of sulfur removed can be as high as 90% to 95%. Because the combustion temperatures inside the boiler are about half of those inside a conventional boiler, nitrogen oxide emissions, which are greater at higher temperatures, are minimized. Furthermore, an FBC boiler increases coal's combustion efficiency and can burn high-, medium-, or low-sulfur coal.

There are two variations on the FBC theme. The first is called *atmospheric fluidized bed combustion* (AFBC). In a bed of inert ash, pulverized coal is thoroughly mixed with sulfur-absorbing limestone. AFBC can cut sulfur dioxide emissions by

85% to 90%. Although its nitrogen oxide reductions are moderate, the atmospheric technique can result in a 10% to 15% increase in electricity generated. In the second variation, *pressurized FBC,* the boiler is pressurized up to 16 times atmospheric pressure. (Atmospheric pressure is the pressure of air at sea level—about 14.7 pounds to the square inch.) Pressurized FBC makes possible a 40% to 50% increase in electricity as well as a 90% to 95% slash in sulfur dioxide and a moderate cut in nitrogen oxides.

Another way to clean coal during incineration is to change it into a liquid or gaseous fuel by exposing it to oxygen under high temperature and pressure. This straightforward process bears the unwieldy name *integrated gasification combined cycle.* Originally developed before World War II, this technique pays huge dividends: a 95% to 99% reduction of sulfur dioxide, a moderate reduction of nitrogen oxides, and a 50% to 150% rise in electricity generated. It also creates as waste a usable slag (residue) and a salable form of sulfur.

There are also two absorbing techniques primarily for sulfur. The first is *furnace sorbent injection* (FSI), in which a sorbent, or absorbing substance, is blasted into the high-temperature region of a furnace during combustion. Sulfur dioxide removal totals 50% to 70%. A cousin to FSI is the *slagging combustor,* which burns coal at temperatures high enough to melt the coal's mineral content into slag. The reductions are slightly higher—50% to 90%—and nitrogen oxide removal is again moderate.

Finally, there are *nitrogen oxide combustion modification* technologies. Put simply, these techniques lower the incineration temperature to lessen nitrogen oxide emissions by about half. If

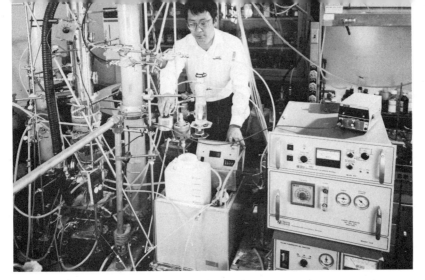

Ted Chang of the Lawrence Berkeley Laboratory in California works on a new scrubber system that removes more than 90% of both sulfur dioxide and nitrogen oxide from power plant emissions and turns these waste gases into commercially useful chemicals.

several of these techniques are used in combination, removal rates can rise to about 70% of nitrogen oxides. These means, however, reduce sulfur dioxide by only about 10% to 20%.

IN THE CHIMNEY

Most procedures for cleaning coal before and during burning are in the experimental stage. By contrast, postcombustion technologies have been around in a number of forms for some time. The most widely used, and seemingly most effective, is known as *flue gas desulfurization*. A smoke-cleaning device fitted to the plant's smokestack, in essence, captures the cat before it is out of the bag. Scrubbers, as these devices are popularly known, are expensive, with price tags of up to $100 million apiece. They also cost a great deal to maintain and operate, and they create large amounts of hazardous waste—scrubber ash—which must then be disposed of properly.

The benefits of scrubbers, however, are undeniable. Late-model scrubbers can comb 90% or more of sulfur dioxide and between 40% and 90% of nitrogen oxides out of waste gas. They are also more reliable and more efficient than the first generation of scrubbers and produce a usable by-product.

Another smokestack solution is called *selective catalytic nitrogen oxide reduction.* Pioneered by the Japanese in the 1970s primarily as an antismog measure, this operation involves shooting ammonia-laden steam or air into the chimney at low temperatures. The chemical reaction that takes place transforms nitrogen oxides—to the tune of 65% to 80%—into elemental nitrogen and water vapor.

Much research and development needs to be done to bring these technologies into marketable form. Yet in the United States, where coal-fired plants are reponsible for 57% of the electric power generated and government forecasts predict that the demand for electric power will grow at an annual rate of 2.4%, clearly these clean coal solutions must be vigorously pursued not only for environmental but for economic reasons. In nations such as China, where the use of coal—the chief fuel for more than a billion people—is expected to double by the year 2000, such means to clean coal will become absolutely vital.

FILTERING OIL

"When Congress talks about clean air these days, it is focusing heavily on the refinery—the jumbled maze of pipes and tanks that stands between 7.5 million barrels of oil a day and 140 million tailpipes." So reported the *New York Times* in May 1990, just days before the House of Representatives passed the new-and-improved Clean Air Act. (The Senate approved it in April, and the president signed it into law in October.)

The reason for such concern is twofold. Every year, these 140 million automobiles—more than 1 car for every 2 persons in the United States—spew into U.S. skies almost half of the more than 50 million tons of pollutants that have been implicated in acid rain. Furthermore, although some technologies, such as scrubbers, can help contain pollution disgorged by petroleum-fired utilities, they do nothing for the pollution coughed from petroleum-fired cars.

Regulations imposed by the original Clean Air Act were a significant step forward. The curbing of lead was the greatest success story: Atmospheric emissions of lead dropped 96%, due in large measure to the mandatory introduction of catalytic converters on automobiles, which are damaged by lead and so virtually require unleaded gas. As a result of converters and new requirements on the amount of lead allowed in gasoline, average lead levels in the blood of U.S. citizens fell by more than one-third between 1976 and 1980, reports the Worldwatch Institute. Catalytic converters, which burn components of gasoline that are incompletely burned in the engine, also reduce hydrocarbons by 87% and nitrogen oxides by 62% over the life of a vehicle.

Yet many environmentalists and legislators felt these strides were not great enough. So in the past decade they have turned their attention to the refinery, where crude oil is processed into gasoline (as well as a host of other petroleum products ranging from lighter fluid to floor wax). Processing begins in a distillation tower: Oil is heated and its vapors rise into the tower. Since chemicals have different boiling points, the various crude-oil components condense back into a liquid at different temperatures and thus at varying heights in the tower. In this way, gas is born.

Before it is trucked to a service station, however, gasoline goes through a host of refinement processes. These result not only in higher octane (which reduces engine "knock") but in more gas per barrel of crude oil. In 1920, using distillation towers only, a 42-gallon barrel of oil yielded 11 gallons of gasoline; using refineries today, that figure has risen to 19 gallons.

But such refinement has come at a cost. The lead added to raise gasoline octane levels wound up in Americans' bloodstreams. Bowing to Clean Air Act regulations, refiners reduced the lead content but, to keep octane high, added substances called aromatics. Like electric utilities and their tall smokestacks, however, refiners were actually replacing one problem with another. Aromatics, it seems, contribute to smog.

The new Clean Air Act calls for a cut in aromatics to 25%, a halving of current levels in superunleaded gas. Refiners complain that this new regulation, along with a host of other mandates designed to significantly reduce pollutants emitted from the tail pipe, will cost them $15 billion to $25 billion over the next decade—costs that will be reflected at the pump. But with public opinion clearly behind the new proposals, refiners have no choice. In fact, some refiners have already put some "reformulated" gasolines on the market.

These technologies—from clean coal to reformulated gas—are not cure-alls. They do little, for example, to decrease the release of carbon dioxide, the most dangerous greenhouse gas, into the atmosphere. "The only way to protect natural resources *and* contain oil imports *and* slow global climate change is to burn much less fossil fuel," wrote the World Resource Institute's James MacKenzie and Mohamed El-Ashry in *Technology Review* (April 1989).

Energy efficiency can work. According to the Worldwatch Institute, the American Council for an Energy-Efficient Economy (ACEEE) has outlined conservation measures that, in an area of the Midwest that is responsible for a third of the country's utility-generated sulfur dioxide, could reduce demand for electricity 15% below utility forecasts. If implemented, this program would slash sulfur dioxide emissions by 7% to 11% between 1992 and 2002 and nitrogen oxides by an unknown but significant amount. The ACEEE also determined that the Midwest could save $4 billion to $8 billion if emissions controls and intensive conservation measures were both pursued as part of a nationwide effort to cut sulfur dioxide emissions by half.

Industry cannot bear the entire burden. Energy-efficiency measures at home are equally vital. Simple things such as turning off lights when leaving a room can add up over time to substantially less fossil fuels burned at the power plant to produce that electricity. Recycling can also work wonders, not just in saving precious landfill space but in preventing pollution. The Worldwatch Institute reports that each ton of paper made from recycled newspapers rather than wood cuts energy use by one-fourth to three-fifths and air pollutants by three-fourths; similarly, aluminum made from recycled cans rather than virgin ore slashes resulting emissions of nitrogen oxides by 95% and sulfur dioxide by 99%.

Another way to burn less fossil fuels is to use a different energy source altogether. Renewable-energy technologies, such as photovoltaic (solar) cells, wind turbines, hydropower, and geothermal energy derived from active volcanoes, still have a long way to go to become commercially viable on a large scale. "But once they are in place," say MacKenzie and El-Ashry, "nonfossil technologies will alleviate a whole range of national problems—not just tree and crop damage but urban air pollution, climate change, and dependency on foreign oil as well."

NEW FUELS FOR CARS

Nearly half of the nitrogen oxides released in this country comes from transportation: cars, trucks, buses, motorcycles,

Cars that run on electricity, such as Daihatsu's experimental Urban Buggy, emit far fewer pollutants than do gasoline-powered vehicles. Because of their high operating cost and other drawbacks, however, they are not yet a viable alternative.

airplanes, and other vehicles. While sulfur dioxide has been on the decrease in this country since 1970, nitrogen oxides have been on the rise because of the sheer number of new cars appearing on U.S. roads each year. The more than 20 million tons of nitrogen oxides these cars spew into American skies annually cause smog to befoul cities and acid rain to fall on the landscape.

How can nitrogen oxides from vehicles be curbed? One proposed way is to introduce alternative fuels, such as methanol, ethanol, natural gas, hydrogen, or electricity. The problem with many of these options is that although they may significantly reduce the pollutants that cause acid rain and smog, they may open a Pandora's box of other dangerous chemicals.

Vehicles that run on methanol, for example, would release far fewer hydrocarbons and nitrogen oxides that produce smog. But compared to cars that run on gasoline, methanol-powered automobiles would emit two to five times more formaldehyde, a probable human carcinogen (cancer-producing substance), says Michael Renner of the Worldwatch Institute. If methanol were fashioned from coal, as it could be if it became a widely used fuel, then emissions of carbon dioxide, the primary greenhouse gas, would be 20% to 160% greater than the amount emitted by using gasoline, according to the World Resources Institute's James MacKenzie. Finally, methanol is extremely poisonous. Small, internal doses, prolonged skin contact, or inhalation may cause blindness.

Two other potential gas substitutes, natural gas and ethanol, only partially solve the problem. According to the California Assembly Office of Research, natural-gas use in cars would reduce hydrocarbons by 40% to 60% and carbon monoxide by 50% to 95% but would increase nitrogen oxides by

Smog blankets a neighborhood of Mexico City, a metropolis well known for its severe and incessant air pollution.

25%—a step in the wrong direction as far as smog and acid rain are concerned. Ethanol, known popularly as grain alcohol, would also not help the smog problem. It releases large amounts of acetaldehyde, a chemical that can speed ozone formation.

In terms of acid rain, the most promising alternative fuels for cars are electricity and hydrogen. The California Assembly Office of Research estimates that autos run on electricity generated by natural gas would shave emissions of nitrogen oxides by 84% as well as hydrocarbons by 99% and carbon monoxide by nearly 100%. There would be other benefits, as well. In a letter to the *New York Times*, Dr. Daniel Berg of Rensselaer Polytechnic Institute wrote, "If 5 percent of the urban miles traveled could be in electrified vehicles by the year 2000, four billion gallons of gasoline would be saved that year, our oil imports would decline by a quarter million barrels per day, and the United States balance of trade would improve by $1.5 billion."

Cars run on hydrogen that is created by solar energy or another pollution-free energy source, calculates the World Resources Institute, would emit no hydrocarbons or carbon monoxide and a significantly lower amount of nitrogen oxides. Yet neither electricity nor hydrogen is ready for commercial use, primarily because the energy needed to produce them either would not solve the problem (in the case of fossil fuels) or is not yet commercially viable (in the case of solar energy, for example).

As is the case with power plants, clearing the air of vehicle pollutants will happen properly only if technological solutions go hand in hand with efficiency measures. Certain countries already have driving restrictions in place. In Italy, the heart of Florence is closed to cars during daylight hours. Similarly, parts of central Rome are off-limits to vehicle traffic during rush hours. In Mexico City, which arguably has the worst urban pollution in the world, one-fifth of cars—based on their license-plate numbers—are prohibited from driving on one day of the five-day business week.

Because only minor curbs to driving have been successful in the United States, another option consumers have is to buy a more efficient car in the first place. And despite the auto industry's claim that fuel economy and reduced emissions are practically a contradiction in terms, both the EPA and the Office of Technology Assessment say they do not have to be. In fact, Chris Calwell of the Natural Resources Defense Council found in a survey of 781 models that the 50 most efficient autos released one-third less hydrocarbons than the average car and about one-half less than the 50 least efficient ones.

Another solution, of course, is for the consumer to impose his or her own restrictions on driving. In many cities, where roads have become overwhelmed by cars in recent years, rush hour is for many commuters a daily nightmare. For these drivers, the relief offered by public transport, biking, or walking to work may have strong appeal regardless of the need to stop acid rain. Carpooling is another individual option that would reduce nitrogen oxide emissions considerably.

All of the solutions discussed so far deal with stopping acid rain before it is born. Since there are few means to combat acids once they have fallen to earth, these technological cures, along with strong government policies and conservation efforts, are essentially the only means countries have available to them. Which strategies nations can and will adopt differ radically, but there is clearly a pressing need for a broad, global effort to combat this growing pollution problem.

All over the world, famous historical structures such as the Washington Monument in Washington, D.C., are suffering damage from acid rain.

G L O B A L   S O L U T I O N S

Humankind has waged the battle against pollution for centuries. The first antipollution decree probably came in 1306, when King Edward I of England forbade London craftsmen from burning "sea coles," chunks of coal that washed up on England's shores. By the early 19th century, the Industrial Revolution had worsened England's air quality considerably. In his book *Hard Times* (1854), Charles Dickens describes what the sky above England's most heavily industrialized cities could be like:

> Coketown lay shrouded in a haze of its own, which appeared impervious to the sun's rays. You only knew the town was there because there could be no such sulky blotch upon the prospect without a town. A blur of soot and smoke, now confusedly tending this way, now that way. . . .

Such serious pollution led to the formation in London of the Coal Smoke Abatement Society, perhaps the world's first antipollution lobbying group. Yet decades after the society's founding, London's pollution problem remained so severe that thousands died there in the 1952 disaster. That tragic event led to stricter emissions regulations, but intensive control of air pollution—not only in England but around the world—did not occur until acid rain's ravages came to be publicly known in the late 1960s.

The first comprehensive pollution control measure came in the United States in 1970, with the passing of the first Clean Air Act. The act came about, in large part, from an enormous swell of public concern born of the first Earth Day. The 1970 act worked small wonders. Between 1970 and 1987, according to the EPA, sulfur dioxide emissions fell by 28% and particulates by 62%.

Despite these gains, many scientists and environmentalists, as previously mentioned, felt that the original Clean Air Act did not go far enough. In order to turn back the tide of destruction that threatened to engulf the nation's waters, forests, soils, and monuments, they argued, far stricter emissions limits on factories, homes, automobiles, and other sources of sulfur and nitrogen oxides must be instituted. After years of deadlock in the government—largely the result of intense lobbying by industry spokespersons who complained of the monumental costs to industry of any stringent new restrictions—President George Bush finally took the initiative. In July 1989, he submitted to Congress his own plan of attack against air pollution. In November 1990, after it passed in both the House and Senate, Bush signed the new Clean Air Act into law.

Stating that every American "deserves to breathe clean air," President Bush announced at a press conference that the U.S. Clean Air Act of 1990 "means cleaner cars, cleaner power plants, cleaner factories, and cleaner fuels. And it means a cleaner America."

President George Bush (seated) signs the 1990 Clean Air Act as EPA Administrator William Reilly (left) and Energy Secretary James Watkins look on.

The new act calls for cuts of sulfur dioxide emissions from fossil-fuel burning by at least 10 million tons (roughly a halving of 1980 levels) and of nitrogen oxide emissions by about 2 million tons per year (an annual drop of about 10% from the 20.4 million tons released in 1980). Because nitrogen oxides cause smog as well as acid rain, the act calls for new controls on tail-pipe emissions and, depending on the severity of a region's smog problem, stricter vehicle emissions tests, the use of vapor-recovery systems at the pump, and the mandatory sale of cleaner-burning fuels. In addition, the bill requires the development of a haze-monitoring network as well as an $8 million 5-year study of the contribution of air pollutants to atmospheric haze.

The 868-page document also authorizes the start of a host of research projects. Some target acid rain's effects on the environment, such as a $6 million study of the impact on Adirondack waters and a new program to monitor the effects on

The Magma Copper Company smelter in San Manuel, Arizona (left), was the scene of a protest against acid rain in 1982, when activists from the environmental group Greenpeace climbed up the left smokestack to unfurl a banner (right) proclaiming, Stop Acid Rain.

entire ecosystems, such as wetlands, forests, and soils. Others are aimed at alternative technologies. These include a study of the pollutants that cleaner-burning fuels would emit and a joint study by the EPA and the Federal Energy Regulatory Commission to determine the ecological savings that renewable energy (such as solar cells) would offer.

The new law also calls for the continuation of the National Acid Precipitation Assessment Program (NAPAP), the $535 million, 10-year federal study that the Bush Administration halted in 1990 after only about 8 years of research. NAPAP will not only continue its measurements of acid rainfall around the country but will maintain a National Acid Lakes Registry to monitor a representative sample of acid-prone lakes.

These new controls and research will not come cheap. The Clean Air Working Group, a coalition of nearly 2,000 energy companies, estimates that when fully implemented, the new act—which also targets the release of toxic chemicals that threaten everything from city dwellers to the ozone layer—could cost taxpayers between $50 billion and $104 billion annually. A similar coalition of environmental groups, known as the National Clean Air Coalition, puts the figure at about $20 billion a year. Yet both groups seem to agree that investments, while staggering, will be worth it in the long run. As Richard Ayers, chairman of the environmental coalition, put it, the new act is "cause for celebration and hope."

Naturally, the U.S. legislation was enthusiastically received in Canada, which had been frustrated by the slow pace of action on the acid rain issue during the Reagan administration and which in 1985 passed legislation to halve its own sulfur dioxide emissions within 10 years.

DEEPER CUTS IN EUROPE

Europe, where acid rain may be taking the most serious toll, has also developed a clean air act. Under the auspices of the UN Economic Commission for Europe, European nations have signed agreements to slash emissions of acid-forming pollutants. Because many European countries are at the mercy of their upwind neighbors, the agreements also take into account the amount of pollution flowing across international boundaries. A 1985 sulfur dioxide accord calls for a 30% reduction (from 1980 levels) of sulfur emissions or the amount of sulfur pollution that blows across national lines by 1993. The nitrogen oxide agreement, signed in 1988, requires a freeze of nitrogen oxide releases at 1987 levels by 1994, as well as further talks aimed at actual reductions.

In November 1988, the European Community went even further. Overall, the community plans to lower sulfur dioxide emissions from 1980 levels at existing power plants by 57% by 2003 and nitrogen oxide emissions by 30% by 1998. Each country in the community will have different restrictions, based on their industrial development, dependence on domestic high-sulfur coal, the amount of pollution they unwittingly export to neighboring states, and other factors.

JAPAN: ANTISMOG PIONEER

Although new controls in both Europe and the United States target sulfur dioxide heavily, many environmentalists feel the restrictions barely scratch the surface when it comes to nitrogen oxides. Not so in Japan, where a health-threatening smog dilemma has forced the government to require plants to remove at least 73% of nitrogen oxides. Japan has been a pioneer in selective catalytic reduction techniques (see Chapter 6), which many other countries have yet to even try. The Japanese have also gone after sulfur, removing 39% of total sulfur dioxide emissions between 1973 and 1984. In the latter year, the Worldwatch Institute reported that Japan had installed scrubbers in more than 1,000 power plants and smelters, compared to only 200 in the

United States. In fact, by 1987, 85% of Japan's coal-fired plants bore scrubbers, compared to 50% in Sweden, 40% in what was then West Germany, and only 20% in the United States.

While Japan leads in emissions cuts, Sweden is thus far the only country to extensively attack pollution after the fact. Perhaps the most enlightened of European nations in its efforts to halt acid rain, Sweden has taken to liming its acidified lakes in a last-ditch effort to revive them. Each year, at a cost of roughly $50 million, Sweden pours huge amounts of acid-neutralizing lime into about 500 Swedish lakes. Liming does return lakes to a neutral state and is relatively inexpensive at about $10 to $15 an acre-foot per year. (An acre-foot refers to the amount needed to cover one acre to a depth of one foot.) The treatment can be costly, however, when applied on a large scale or in remote areas where lime must be applied by helicopter. Also, whether aquatic life can permanently return to these waters is still uncertain. At any rate, liming is only a stopgap measure that is no substitute for energy efficiency and emissions cuts.

FRIENDLY NEIGHBORS

Sweden has found yet another means to reduce acid rain within its borders. Because 89% of the sulfur that is poisoning its lakes comes from other countries, including a large dose from those in Eastern Europe, the Swedish government has decided to get to the root of the problem. Over a 3-year period in the early 1990s, Sweden will provide $45 million in aid to Poland, its highly polluting neighbor just across the Baltic Sea. Most of this aid will fund environmental protection projects.

Liming can neutralize acidic waters but is only a temporary cure—as well as an expensive one.

Other European countries also feel that helping neighboring lands solve their pollution problems may be more effective than further cuts at home. In a boldly original plan, the Netherlands Electricity Generating Board will spend $35 million to finance a desulfurization plant in Poland to reduce the amount of sulfur spewed from that country's antiquated power stations. According to Irene Carsouw, a spokeswoman for the board, the Netherlands already combs 92% of sulfur from its own emissions. Investing $35 million there would remove perhaps a few percent more, amounting to about 6,000 tons of sulfur, she says. By contrast, the new Polish plant will help remove 45,000 tons of sulfur from emissions in Poland, which relies on a domestic supply of high-sulfur brown coal.

Experts feel that such aid by wealthy and highly industrialized nations is absolutely necessary to help Eastern Europe and the Soviet Union become environmentally responsible. Following World War II, the Soviet Union and its Warsaw Pact allies underwent rapid industrialization to, in essence, catch up with the West. Yet they built virtually no pollution controls into their factories and power stations, which relied—and continue to rely—on the high-sulfur brown coal that is abundant in the region. These countries have neither the technology nor the capital to purchase the technology needed to limit the vast amounts of pollution emitted by their out-of-date equipment.

Besides the Swedish and Dutch aid packages, several other promising initiatives are under way. In a limited yet symbolic move, the U.S. Congress has allocated $40 million to help Poland and Hungary with environmental troubles. Two U.S. based organizations, the Rocky Mountain Institute and the Natural Resource Defense Council, are advising the Soviet government on how to improve energy efficiency in the Soviet Union.

Before they became one nation in 1990, East and West Germany pledged to help each other control pollution. In 1988, the 2 countries agreed that East Germany would provide 120 million marks ($65 million at then-current exchange rates) and West Germany 300 million marks ($163 million) to acquire the latest in coal-burning equipment and antipollution technologies over a 3-year period.

Such international cooperation and aid is even more vital to help Third World nations combat their escalating air pollution woes. Pollution experts are extremely concerned about these underdeveloped countries, where the greatest rise in population in the coming decades will trigger increased urbanization and industrialization—and thus pollution.

Many international organizations and government agencies have begun ambitious programs to help the Third World. According to the Worldwatch Institute report *Clearing the Air: A Global Agenda*, the World Bank aims to increase its air-pollution initiatives; the International Environment Bureau in Switzerland and the World Environment Center in New York are helping to transfer antipollution technology and data to underdeveloped countries; and recent legislation in the U.S. Congress stipulates that the U.S. Agency for International Development encourage energy efficiency and renewable energy technologies through its programs.

As in Eastern Europe and the Soviet Union, low-interest loans can give underdeveloped nations the money they need to begin solving their pollution problems. In 1990, Japan announced that it would lend the Mexican government $850 million to remove sulfur from diesel fuel and heavy fuel oil burned in Mexico, among other antipollution measures. The loan was the first expenditure of a $2-billion fund the Japanese government has set up to help poorer nations with environmental woes.

Mexico, in fact, is at the forefront of a trend that has to begin in Third World countries if air pollution and acid rain are to be checked: taking the problem into one's own hands. As part of a comprehensive $2.5-billion pollution plan announced in October 1990, the Mexican government, reports the *New York Times*, has banned all cars from a 50-square-block area around Mexico City's historic central square, the Zócalo, the most highly polluted section of the most highly polluted city in the world. In addition, the government will replace all 3,500 exhaust-belching city buses with improved models and will require catalytic converters on all 1991 cars.

The sharing of technology and funds by wealthier nations with poorer ones, combined with initiatives within these less developed countries, will help the global community curb acid rain. The sooner this pollution problem is attacked on a wide front, the better the chances of halting the increasing acidification of the earth's soils, forests, and waterways and of purifying the water upon which life on this planet depends.

APPENDIX: FOR MORE INFORMATION

The Acid Rain Foundation
1630 Blackhawk Hills
St. Paul, MN 55122
(919) 828-9443

Acid Rain Information
   Clearinghouse Library
Center for Environmental
   Information, Inc.
33 South Washington Street
Rochester, NY 14608
(716) 271-3550

American Forestry Association
1516 P Street NW
Washington, DC 20005
(202) 667-3300

Canadian Coalition on Acid Rain
112 St. Clair Ave. NW, Suite 401
Toronto, Ontario M4V 2Y3
Canada
(416) 968-2135

Canadian Wildlife Federation
1673 Carling Avenue, Suite 106
Ottawa, Ontario K2A 1C4
Canada
(613) 725-2191

The Conservation Foundation
1250 24th Street NW
Washington, DC 20037
(202) 293-4800

Department of the Interior
U.S. Fish & Wildlife Service
National Ecology Center
Leetown, Box 705
Kearneysville, WV 25430
(304) 725-2061

Electric Power Research Institute
3412 Hillview Avenue
Box 10412
Palo Alto, CA 94303
(415) 855-2000

Environmental Defense
   Fund
257 Park Avenue South
New York, NY 10010
(212) 505-2100

Environmental Protection
   Agency (EPA)
401 M Street SW
Washington, DC 20460
(202) 382-2090

Izaak Walton League of
  America
Level B, 1401 Wilson Blvd.
Arlington, VA 22209
(703) 528-1818

National Academy of Sciences/
  National Research Council
Attn: Environmental Studies
  Board
2010 Constitution Avenue NW
Washington, DC 20418
(202) 452-9592

National Acid Precipitation
  Assessment Program
Program Coordination Office
722 Jackson Place NW
Washington, DC 20506

National Audubon Society
950 Third Avenue
New York, NY 10022
(212) 832-3200

National Clean Air Coalition
530 7th Street SE
Washington, DC 20003
(202) 797-5436

National Wildlife Federation
1412 16th Street NW
Washington, DC 20036
(202) 797-6800

Natural Resources Defense
  Council
40 West 20th Street
New York, NY 10011
(212) 727-2700

Pollution Probe Foundation
12 Madison Avenue
Toronto, Ontario M5R 2S1
Canada
(416) 926-1907

Sierra Club
730 Polk Street
San Francisco, CA 94109
(415) 776-2211

Trout Unlimited
118 Park Street
Vienna, VA 22180
(703) 281-1100

World Resources
  Institute
1709 New York Avenue NW
Washington, DC 20006
(202) 638-6300

Worldwatch Institute
1776 Massachusetts Avenue NW
Washington, DC 20036
(202) 452-1999

World Wildlife Fund
1250 24th Street NW
Washington, DC 20037
(202) 293-4800

FURTHER READING

Ambio 18, no. 3 (1989). Issue devoted to air pollution and acid rain.

Boyle, Robert H., and R. Alexander Boyle. *Acid Rain.* New York: Schocken Books, 1983.

Economic Commission for Europe (ECE). *Air Pollution Across Boundaries.* New York: United Nations, 1985.

Edison Electric Institute. "The Promise of Clean Coal Technology." *Trilogy* (Spring/Summer 1990).

Fisher, Diane, et al. *Polluted Coastal Waters: The Role of Acid Rain.* New York: Environmental Defense Fund, 1988.

French, Hilary F. "Clearing the Air." In *State of the World 1990,* Edited by Linda Starke. New York: Norton, 1990.

Geller, Howard S. *Acid Rain and Electricity Conservation.* Washington, DC: American Council for an Energy-Efficient Economy/Energy Conservation Coalition, 1987.

Howard, Ross, and Michael Perley. *Acid Rain, the North American Forecast.* Toronto: House of Anansi Press, 1980.

Likens, Gene E., et al. "Acid Rain." *Scientific American* 241 (1979): 43–51.

McCormick, John. *Acid Earth: The Global Threat of Acid Pollution.* London: International Institute for Environment and Development, 1985.

MacKenzie, James, and Mohamed T. El-Ashry, *Ill Winds: Airborne Pollution's Toll on Trees and Crops*. Washington, DC: World Resources Institute, 1988.

Mohnen, Volker A. "The Challenge of Acid Rain." *Scientific American* 259 (1988): 30–38.

National Acid Precipitation Assessment Program (NAPAP). *Interim Assessment: The Causes and Effects of Acidic Deposition*, vol. 4. Washington, DC: Government Printing Office, 1987.

Postel, Sandra. *Air Pollution, Acid Rain, and the Future of Forests*. Worldwatch Paper 58. Washington, DC: Worldwatch Institute, 1984.

Renner, Michael. *Rethinking the Role of the Automobile*. Worldwatch Paper 84. Washington, DC: Worldwatch Institute, 1988.

Roth, Philip, et al. *The American West's Acid Rain Test*. Washington, DC: World Resources Institute, 1985.

Speth, James G. *Environmental Pollution: A Long-term Perspective*. Washington, DC: World Resources Institute, 1988.

PICTURE CREDITS

GLOSSARY

acid deposition   The scientific term for **acid rain**; most widely accepted because it takes into account all forms of acid precipitation as well as **dry deposition.**

acidic   Having a **pH** of less than 7. See pH.

acidification   The process of making lakes, forests, or other aquatic or terrestrial ecosystems excessively acidic through **acid deposition.**

acid rain   Precipitation, such as rain, snow, hail, sleet, fog, and dew, or dry deposition, that contains **sulfuric** or **nitric acids** formed in the atmosphere from the burning of **fossil fuels.**

alkaline   Having a pH of more than 7. See pH.

biomass   Plant or animal matter used as fuel; also used to refer to the total weight of living matter in a given area.

black crust   A dark deposit caused by particulates that often collects on buildings in industrialized areas.

buffering capacity   The ability of soil or bodies of water to naturally neutralize acids; also known as **neutralizing capacity.**

clean coal technologies   Various means, many still experimental, to remove pollutants from coal before and during combustion.

cold hardening   The process initiated by a tree's roots in which water is removed from needles or leaves in preparation for the freezing temperatures of winter.

dry deposition   The process in which dry, acidic particles fall to earth, sometimes adhering to plants or structures at ground level.

electrostatic precipitator   A device used in electric power plants to remove **particulates.**

ethanol   Also known as ethyl or grain alcohol, a potential alternative fuel for cars.

flue gas desulfurization   A process in which a scrubber, or chimney filter, removes **sulfur** and **nitrogen oxide** gases from flue gas.

fluidized bed combustion (FBC)   Clean-coal technology that removes sulfur dioxide during combustion by mixing pulverized coal and sulfur dioxide–absorbing limestone; variations include atmospheric FBC and pressurized FBC.

fossil fuels   Coal, petroleum, natural gas, and other products formed deep underground from the remains of living things; the process occurs over millions of years and under intense temperatures and geologic pressure.

furnace sorbent injection   Clean-coal technology in which an absorbing substance, or sorbent, is blown into a furnace to absorb sulfur dioxide.

hydrocarbon   Organic substance consisting of carbon and hydrogen that is often found within coal, petroleum, and natural gas; hydrocarbons emitted from cars are a prime culprit in the formation of **smog.**

integrated gasification combined cycle   Clean-coal technology to remove pollutants from coal by changing the fuel into a liquid or gas under high temperature and pressure during incineration.

methane (CH_4)   A colorless, odorless **hydrocarbon** gas that is the chief component of natural gas.

methanol   Also known as methyl alcohol or wood alcohol, a wood-based or synthetically made substance that is now under consideration as an alternative fuel for cars.

neutralizing capacity   See **buffering capacity**.

nitrate (NO$_3$)   A chemical salt that, with hydrogen, makes up nitric acid and is often used as a plant fertilizer.

nitrogen oxides (NO$_x$)   Any of several oxides of nitrogen that, with sulfur dioxide, are the chief precursors to acid rain.

nitric acid (HNO$_3$)   An acidic chemical, created in the atmosphere from nitrogen oxides, that is a principal constituent of acid rain.

oxidize   To transform by combining with oxygen.

ozone (O$_3$)   The chemical formed when a molecule and an atom of oxygen combine; stratospheric ozone protects living things from ultraviolet radiation from the sun, but ground-level ozone, or photochemical smog, can harm plants and animals.

particulates   A varying mixture of pollutants in solid particle or liquid droplet form released from industrial sources and automobiles and having potentially serious health effects when inhaled.

pH   Literally, potential of Hydrogen; a measure of the alkalinity or acidity of a substance, based on the concentration of hydrogen ions (H$^+$) relative to hydroxyl ions (OH$^-$); on the 14-point pH scale, above 7 (neutral) is alkaline, below 7 is acidic. The scale is logarithmic, e.g., rain with a pH of 4 is 10 times as acidic as rain with a pH of 5.

scrubber   A device used in **flue gas desulfurization** to remove pollutant gases as they waft up a chimney after combustion of fossil fuels.

smelting   The process of separating a metal from its ore.

smog   A term derived from *smoke* and *fog*; haze produced from the reaction of nitrogen oxides and hydrocarbons with sunlight.

sulfate (SO$_4^-$)   A chemical salt that, with hydrogen, makes up sulfuric acid.

sulfur dioxide (SO$_2$)   A toxic pollutant emitted primarily from coal-fired electric power plants and that, along with nitrogen oxides, is a chief precursor to acid rain.

sulfuric acid (H$_2$SO$_4$)   Also called oil of vitriol, a highly corrosive acid that is a principal constituent of acid rain.

Waldsterben   Literally, "forest death" in German; a phenomenon, first documented in Germany, in which acid rain, believed to work in conjunction with other environmental stresses, kills entire forests.

C o n v e r s i o n   T a b l e

(From U.S./English system units to metric system units)

Length

1 inch = 2.54 centimeters
1 foot = 0.305 meters
1 yard = 0.91 meters
1 statute mile = 1.6 kilometers (km.)

Area

1 square yard = 0.84 square meters
1 acre = 0.405 hectares
1 square mile = 2.59 square km.

Liquid Measure

1 fluid ounce = 0.03 liters
1 pint (U.S.) = 0.47 liters
1 quart (U.S.) = 0.95 liters
1 gallon (U.S.) = 3.78 liters

Weight and Mass

1 ounce = 28.35 grams
1 pound = 0.45 kilograms
1 ton = 0.91 metric tons

Temperature

1 degree Fahrenheit = 0.56 degrees Celsius or Centigrade, but to convert from actual Fahrenheit scale measurements to Celsius, subtract 32 from the Fahrenheit reading, multiply the result by 5, and then divide by 9. For example, to convert 212° F to Celsius:

$212 - 32 = 180$ x $5 = 900 \div 9 = 100°$ C

INDEX

Photovoltaic cells, 99
pH scale, 20–22, 51, 66
Pocono Mountains, 44, 52, 63
Poland, 26, 80, 111–13
Pollution control
    in Europe, 109–10, 111–13
    in Japan, 110–11
    in the Third World,114–15
    in the United States, 106–9
Portugal, 79
Postel, Sandra, 73
Potassium, 41
Prague, Czechoslovakia, 80

Quabbin Reservoir, 65

Rainforest destruction, 85–86
Recycling, 98–99
Rocky Mountains, 26, 68–69
Rome, Italy, 16, 102

Saudi Arabia, 26
Scandinavia, 75
Scotland, 77
Scrubbers, 94–95
Seattle, Washington, 69
Selective catalytic nitrogen oxide
    reduction, 95
Shenyang, China, 83
Sichuan, China, 82
Slagging combustor, 93
Smelting, 33
Smith, Charles Angus, 16
Smokestacks, 30–32, 94–95
South Africa, 26
Soviet Union, 15, 26, 27,
    81–82, 113
Soybeans, 47, 67
Spain, 79

Statue of Liberty, 58
Steudler, Paul, 50–51
Sulfation, 56
Sulfur, 27, 28, 29
Sulfuric acid, 16, 28, 31, 36, 42, 57
Sulfur trioxide, 56
Sweden, 15, 17, 32, 75, 79, 111
Switzerland, 32, 78, 79

Temple of the Frescoes,
    Mexico, 58
Third World, 83–87, 114–15
"Thousand Lakes Survey," 76–77
Transboundary problem, 32

United Nations Economic
    Commission for Europe (ECE),
    23, 75, 79
United Nations Environment
    Program, 56, 83, 90

Venezuela, 26, 85
Volcanoes, 26, 28

Waldsterben (forest death), 78–79
Wales, 77
Washington Monument, 58
White, Robert, 45–46
Wildlife, 63–64
Wind turbines, 99
World Health Organization, 56,
    83, 90

Xi'an, China, 83

Yucatán Peninsula, 58
Yugoslavia, 81

Zaire, 86
Zhiyuan, Chen, 82

ABOUT THE AUTHOR

PETER TYSON is managing editor of *Earthwatch* magazine. In 1990 he joined a scientific expedition to Alaska's North Slope to gather evidence of acid rain that is believed to blow into the Arctic from Eurasia, and he has since published articles on acid rain in *Earthwatch*, the *Boston Globe*, and *Arctic Circle* magazine. Formerly an assistant editor at *Omni* magazine, he has been a science writer for nine years.

ABOUT THE EDITOR

RUSSELL E. TRAIN, currently chairman of the board of directors of the World Wildlife Fund and The Conservation Foundation, has had a long and distinguished career of government service under three presidents. In 1957 President Eisenhower appointed him a judge of the United States Tax Court. He served Lyndon Johnson on the National Water Commission. Under Richard Nixon he became under secretary of the Interior and, in 1970, first chairman of the Council on Environmental Quality. From 1973 to 1977 he served as administrator of the Environmental Protection Agency. Train is also a trustee or director of the African Wildlife Foundation; the Alliance to Save Energy; the American Conservation Association; Citizens for Ocean Law; Clean Sites, Inc.; the Elizabeth Haub Foundation; the King Mahendra Trust for Nature Conservation (Nepal); Resources for the Future; the Rockefeller Brothers Fund; the Scientists' Institute for Public Information; the World Resources Institute; and Union Carbide and Applied Energy Services, Inc. Train is a graduate of Princeton and Columbia Universities, a veteran of World War II, and currently resides in the District of Columbia.